The Easy Piano Christmas Collection

Arranged by Bill Boyd

T0055359

ISBN 978-0-634-04753-4

HAL•LEONARD® CORPORATION
7777 W. BLUEMOUND RD. P.O. BOX 13819 MILWAUKEE, WI 53213

Visit Hal Leonard Online at
www.halleonard.com

ontents

AWAY IN A MANGER

Traditional
Words by JOHN T. McFARLAND (v.3)
Music by JAMES R. MURRAY

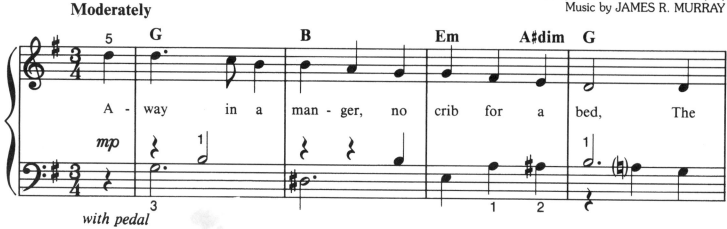

A - way in a man - ger, no crib for a bed, The

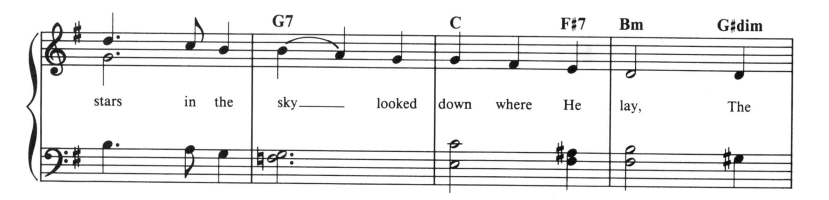

lit - tle Lord Je - sus laid down His sweet head. The

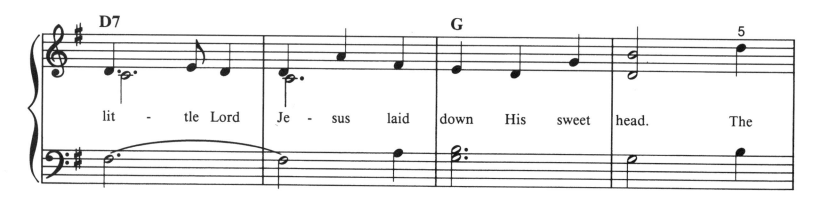

stars in the sky___ looked down where He lay, The

lit - tle Lord Je - sus, a - sleep on the hay. The

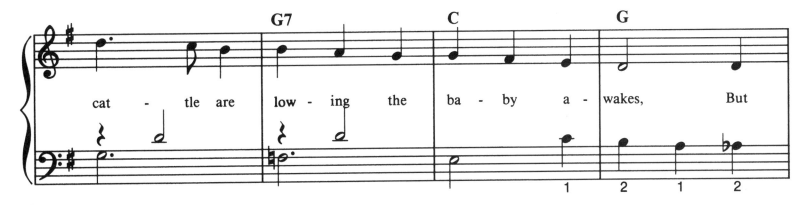

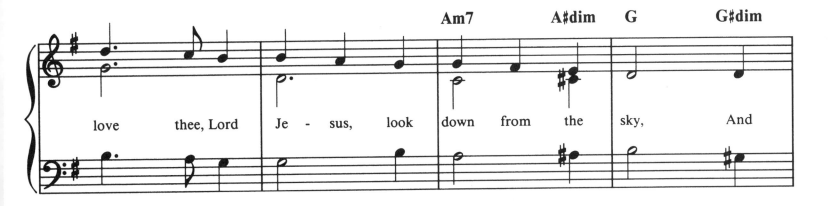

AWAY IN A MANGER

Anonymous Text (vv.1,2)
Text by JOHN T. McFARLAND (v.3)
Music by JONATHAN E. SPILLMAN

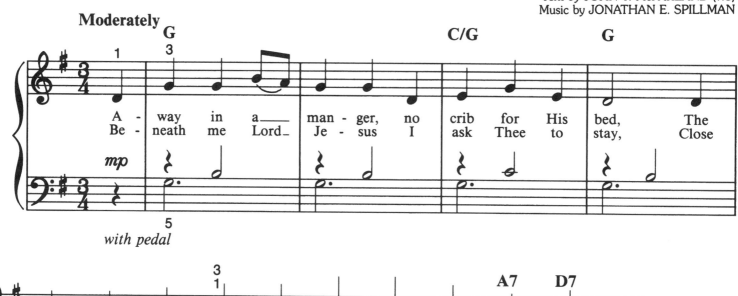

with pedal

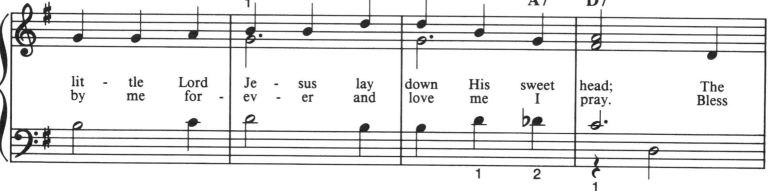

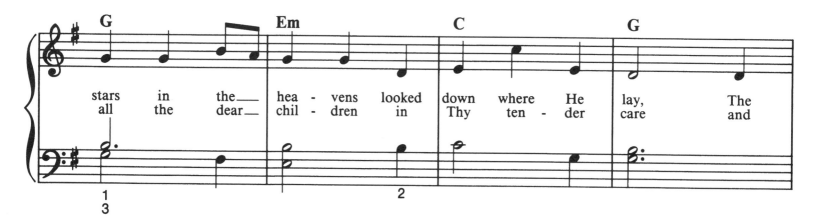

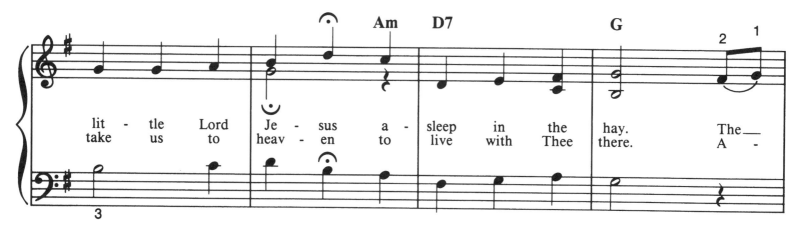

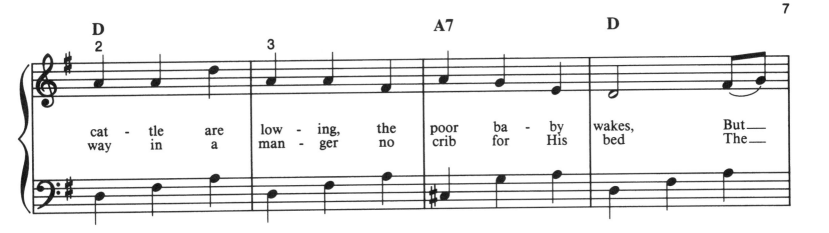

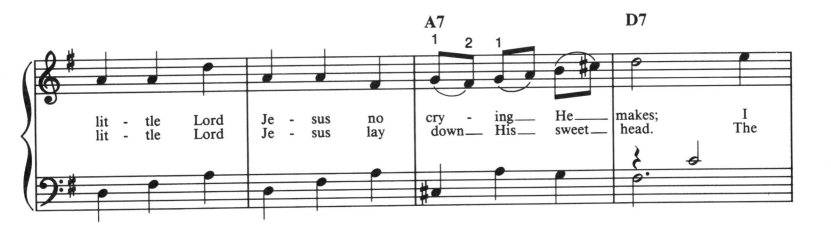

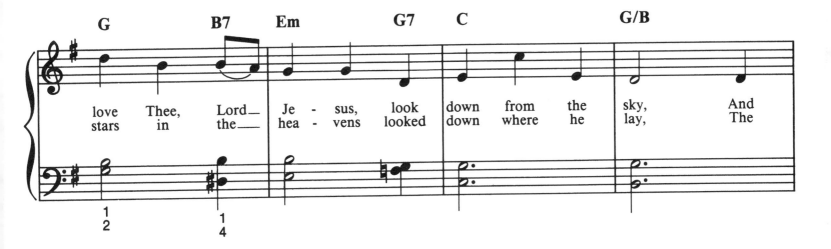

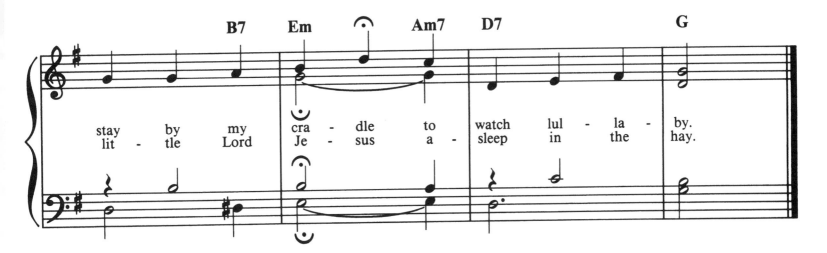

THE BOAR'S HEAD CAROL

Traditional English

With spirit

mf

rit.

a tempo

The boar's head in

with pedal

hand bear I, Be - decked with bays and rose - ma - ry. And I

pray you, my mas - ters mer - ry be, Quot es - tes in con -

vi - vi - o, Ca - put a - pri de - fe - ro, Re - dens lau - des

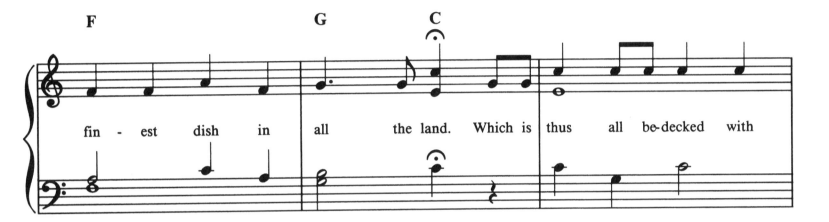

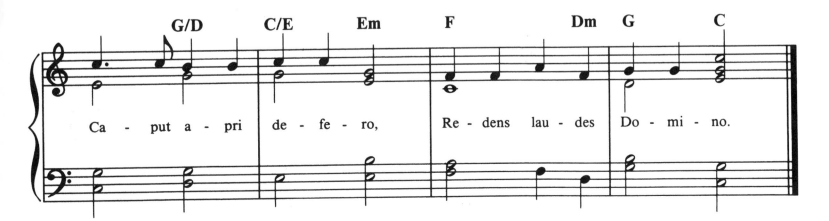

BRING A TORCH, JEANNETTE, ISABELLA

17th Century French Provençal Carol

Moderately

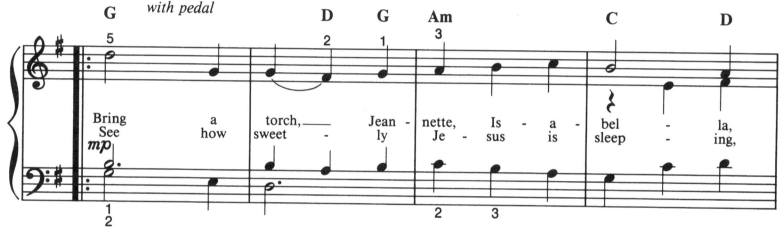

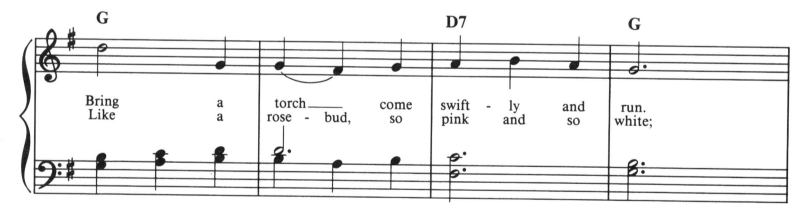

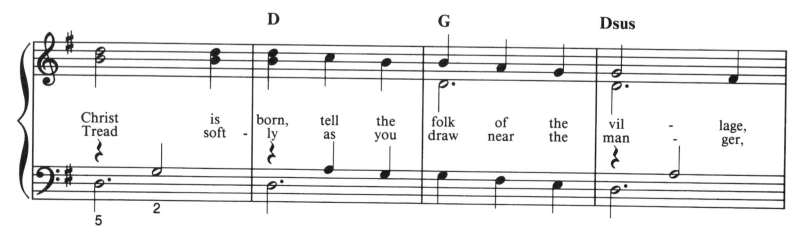

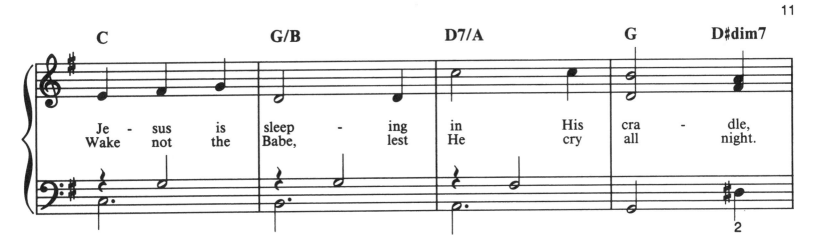

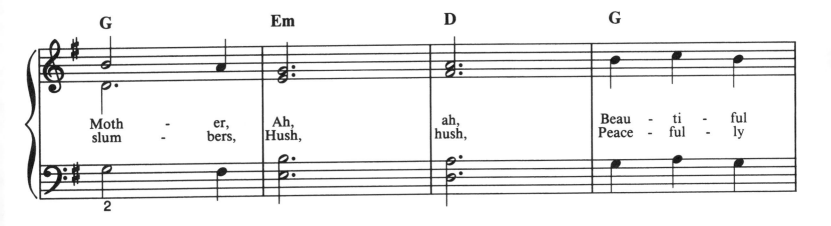

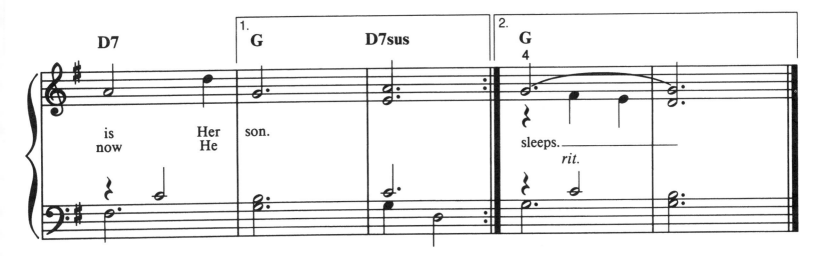

THE CHIPMUNK SONG

Both hands may be played one octave higher than written.

Words and Music by
ROSS BAGDASARIAN

With Pedal

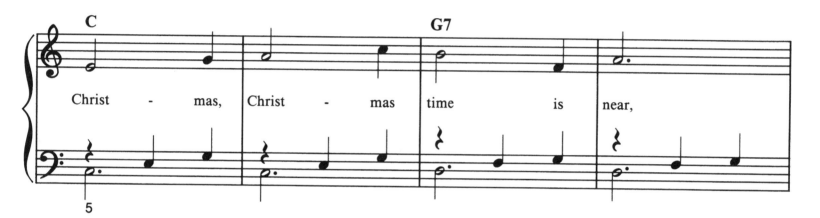

Christ - mas, Christ - mas time is near,

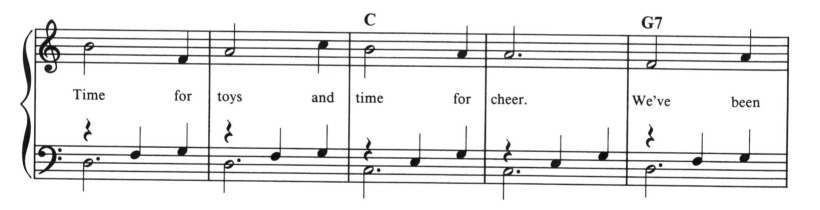

Time for toys and time for cheer. We've been

good but we can't last, Hur - ry Christ - mas,

13

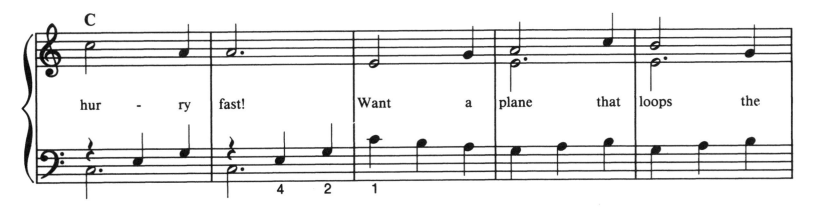

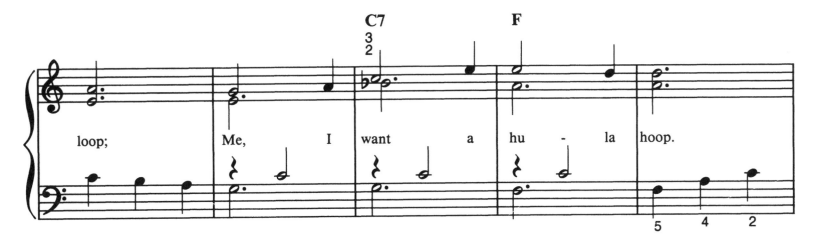

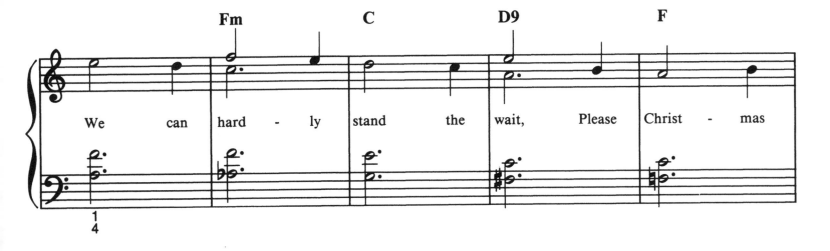

THE CHRISTMAS SONG
(Chestnuts Roasting on an Open Fire)

Music and Lyric by MEL TORME
and ROBERT WELLS

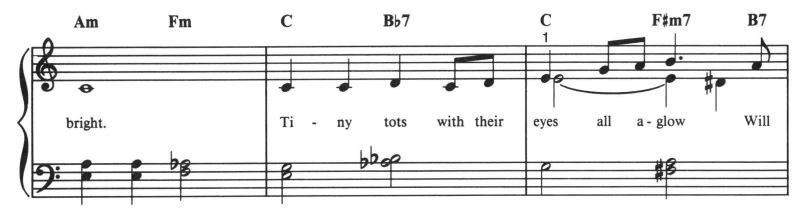

bright. Ti - ny tots with their eyes all a - glow Will

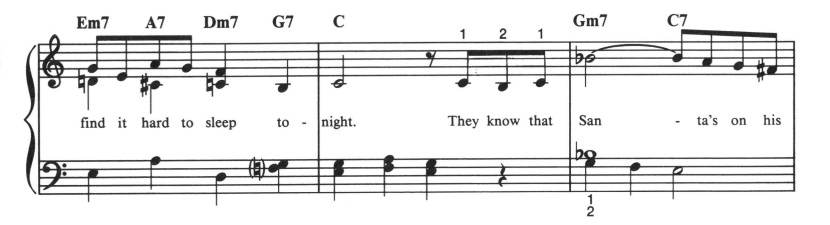

find it hard to sleep to - night. They know that San - ta's on his

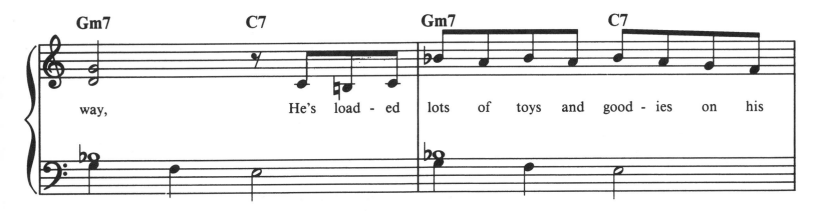

way, He's load - ed lots of toys and good - ies on his

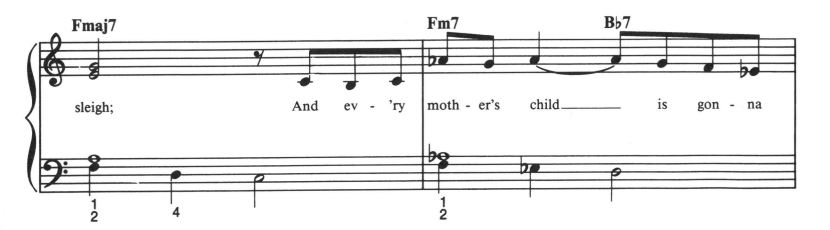

sleigh; And ev - 'ry moth - er's child_____ is gon - na

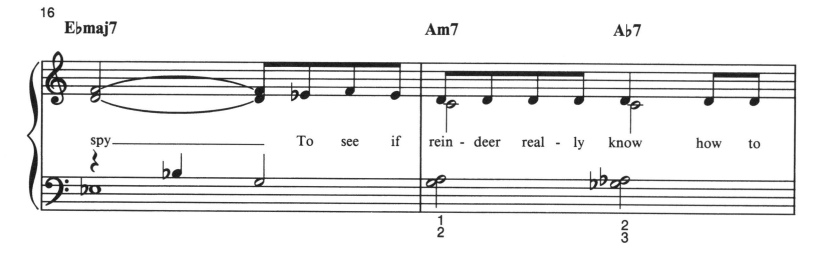

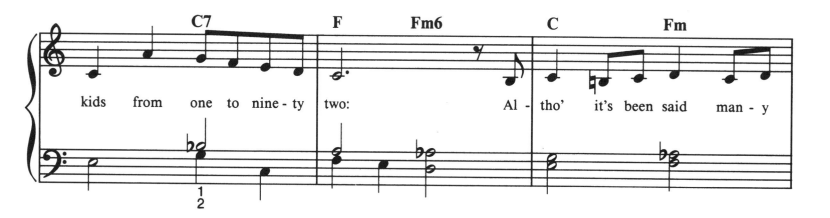

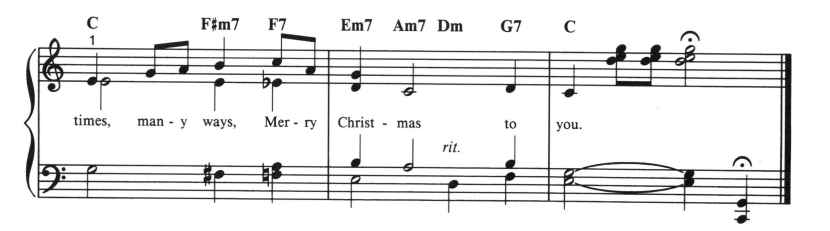

THE CHRISTMAS WALTZ

Words by SAMMY CAHN
Music by JULE STYNE

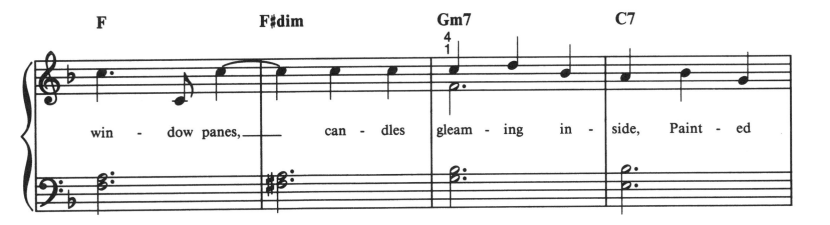

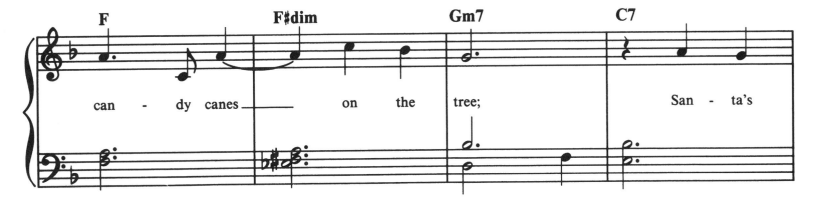

18

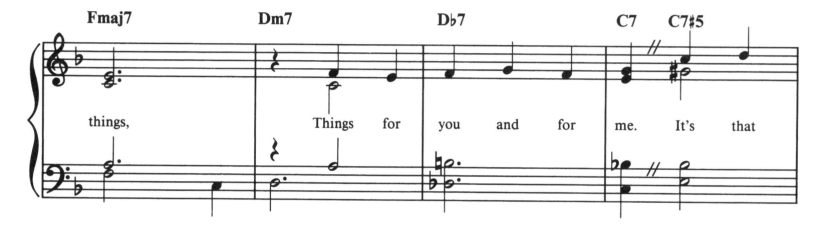

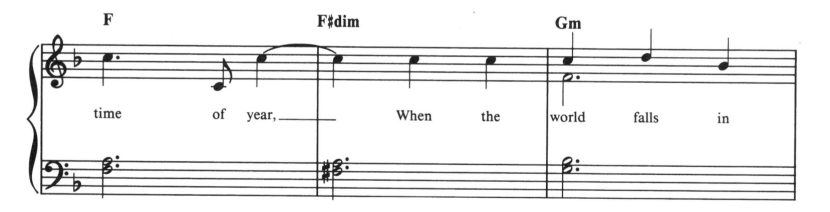

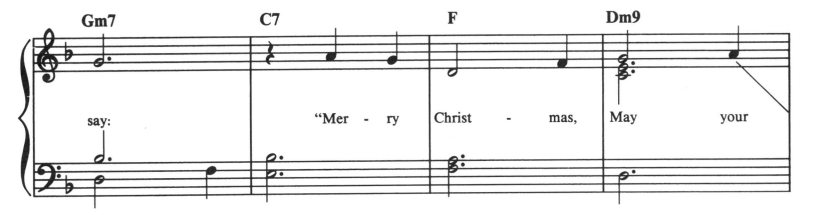

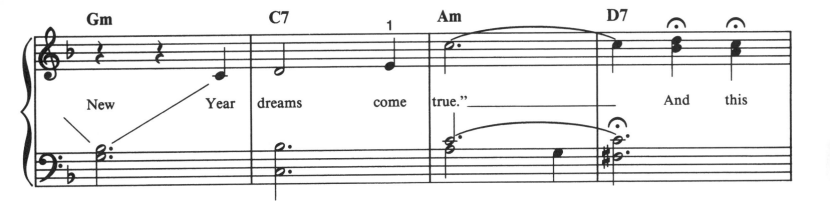

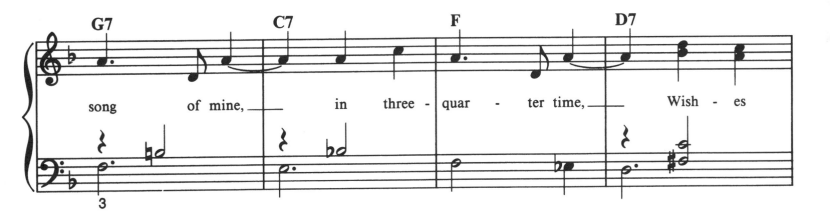

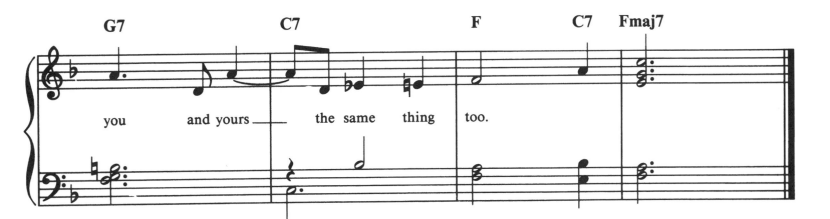

CHRISTMAS TIME IS HERE

from A CHARLIE BROWN CHRISTMAS

Words by LEE MENDELSON
Music by VINCE GUARALDI

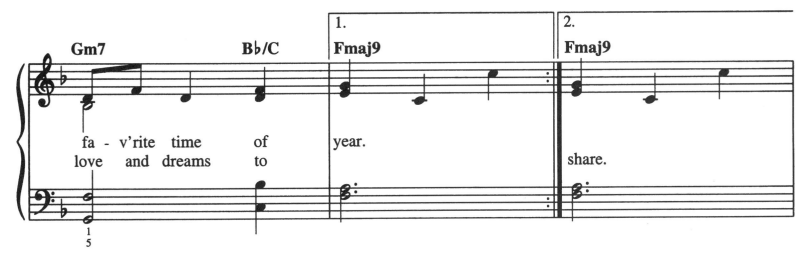

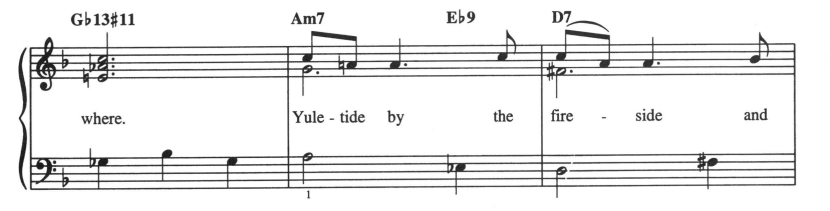

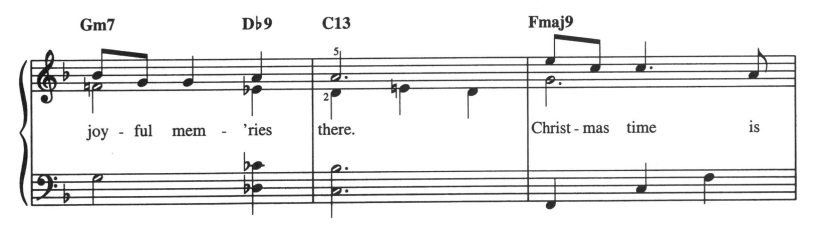

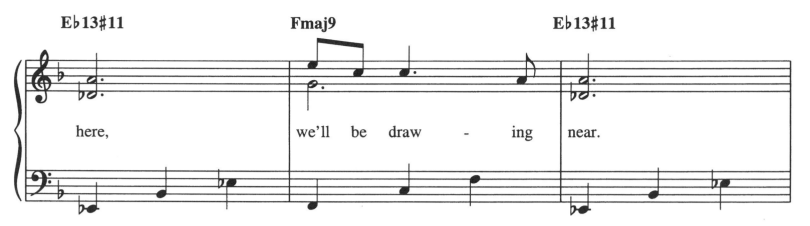

Eb13#11   Fmaj9   Eb13#11

here,   we'll be draw - ing near.

To Coda ⊕

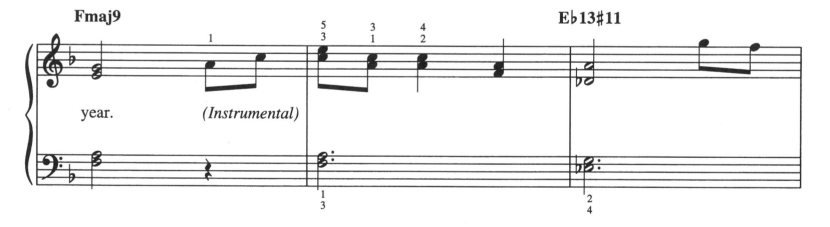

Bm7b5   Am7   Abm7   Gm7   Bb/C

Oh, that we   could al - ways see   such   spir - it through the

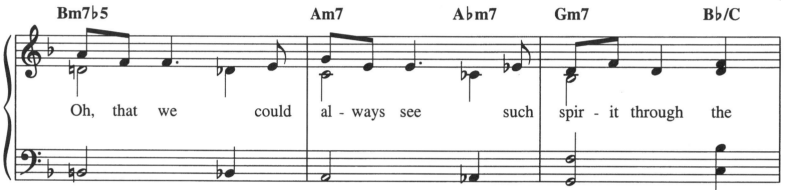

Fmaj9   Eb13#11

year.   *(Instrumental)*

Fmaj9   Eb13#11   Bm7b5   Bbm7

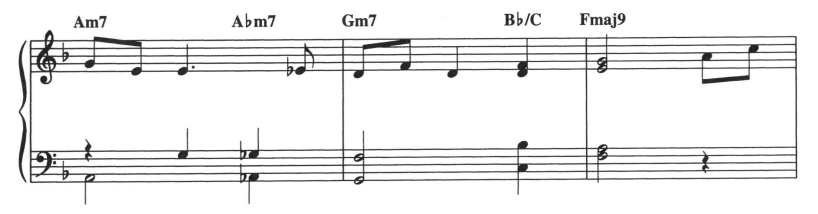

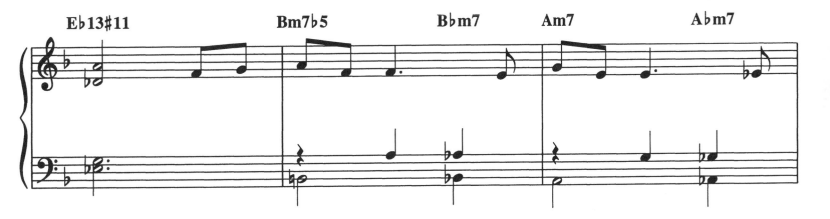

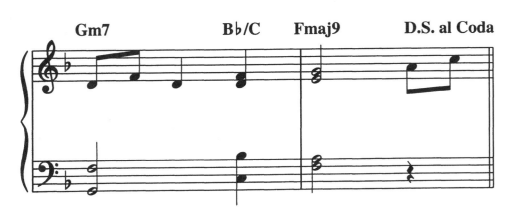

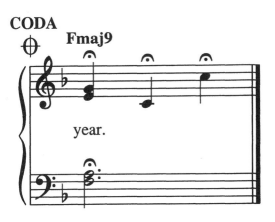

COVENTRY CAROL

Words by ROBERT CROO
Traditional English Melody

Moderately slow

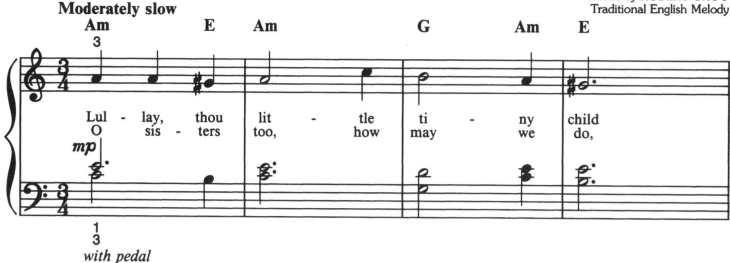

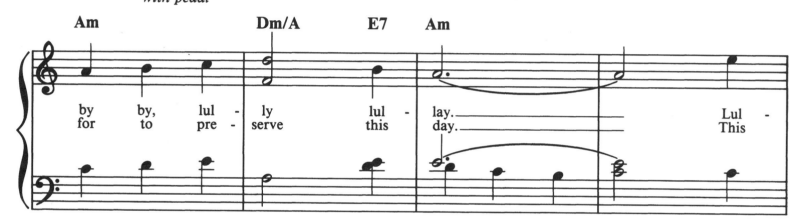

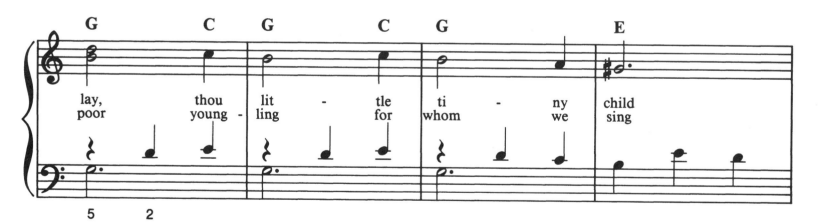

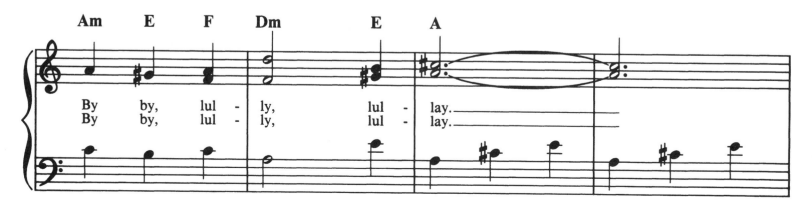

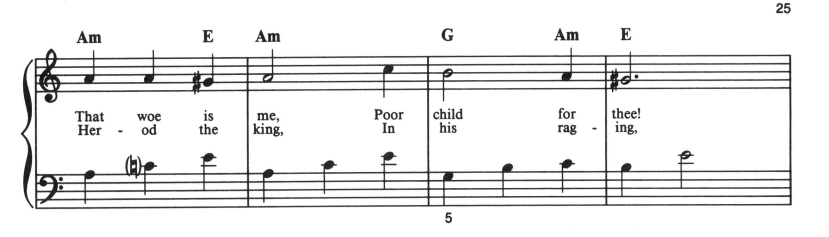

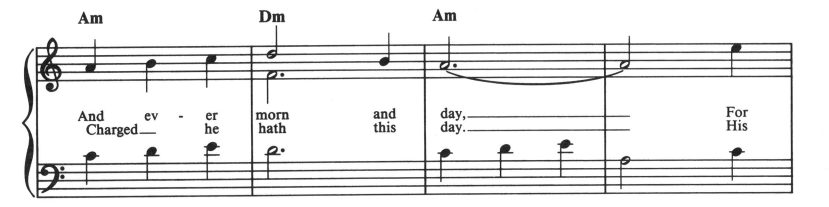

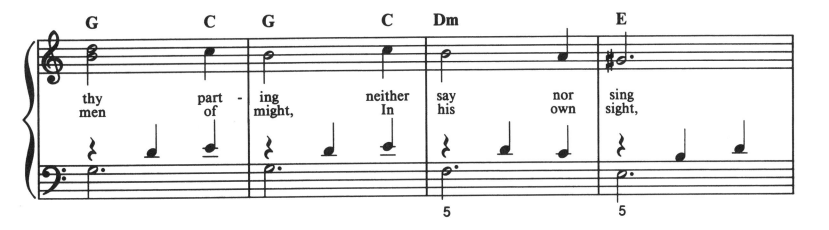

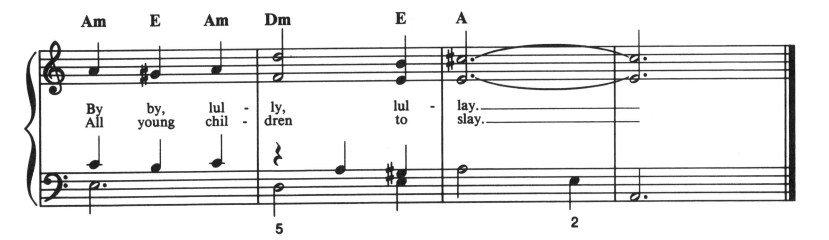

DECK THE HALL

Traditional Welsh Carol

Moderately

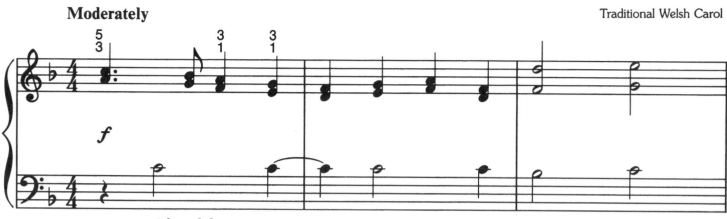

f

with pedal

mf

Deck the hall with boughs of hol - ly,
See the blaz - ing yule be - fore us,

Fa la la la la, la la la la la. 'Tis the sea - son
Fa la la la la, la la la la la. Strike the harp and

to be jol - ly, Fa la la la la, la la la la la.
join the cho - rus. Fa la la la la, la la la la la.

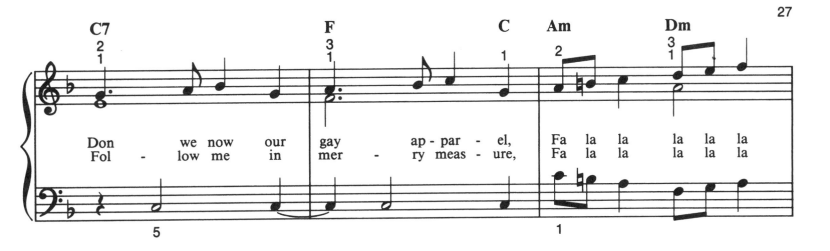

Don - we now our gay ap-par - el,
Fol - low me in mer - ry meas - ure,
Fa la la la la la la
Fa la la la la la la

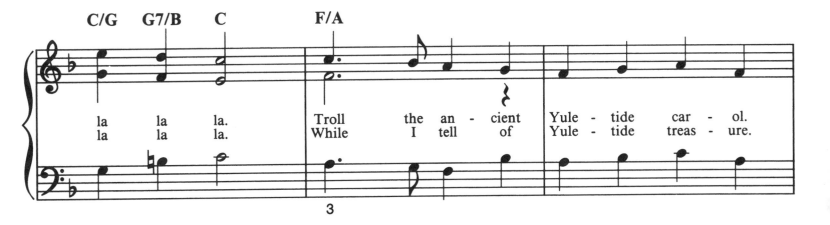

la la la.
la la la.
Troll the an - cient Yule - tide car - ol.
While I tell of Yule - tide treas - ure.

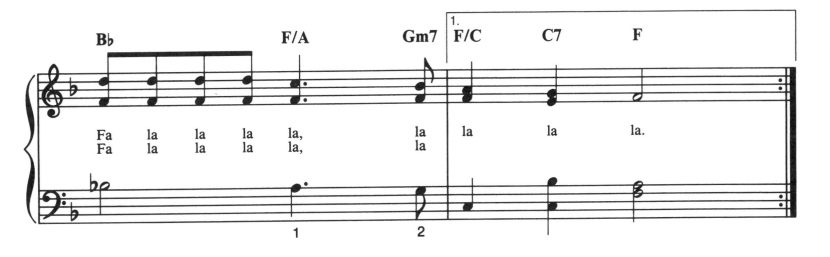

Fa la la la la la, la la la la.
Fa la la la la la, la la

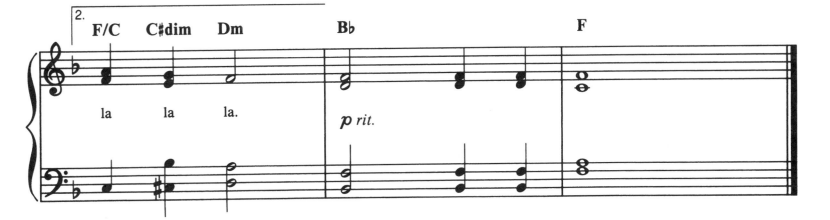

la la la.
p rit.

THE FIRST NOËL

Moderately

17th Century English Carol
Music from W. Sandys' *Christmas Carols*

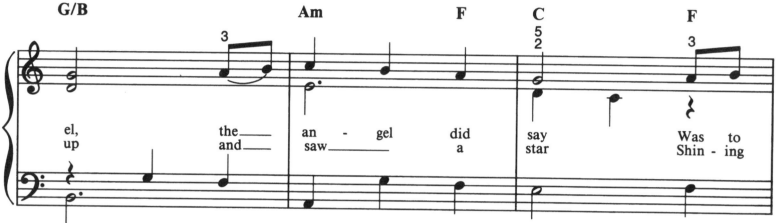

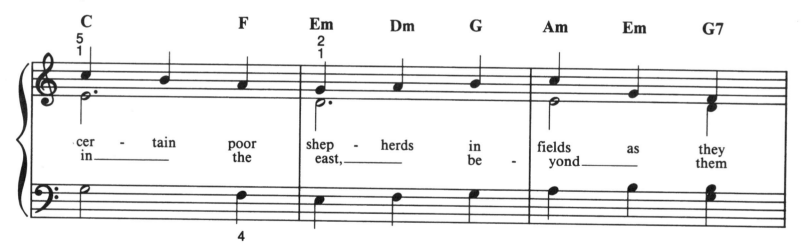

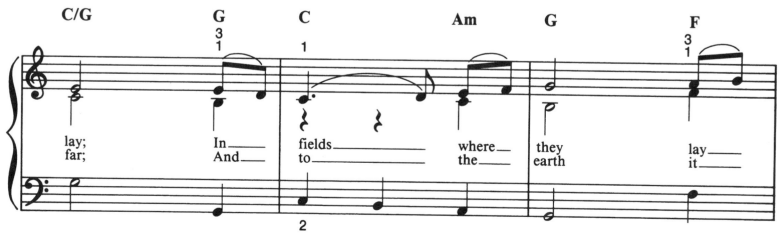

29

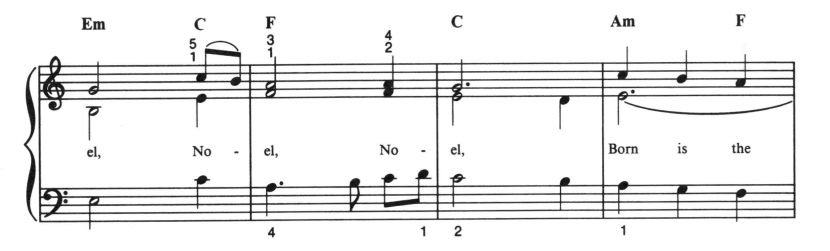

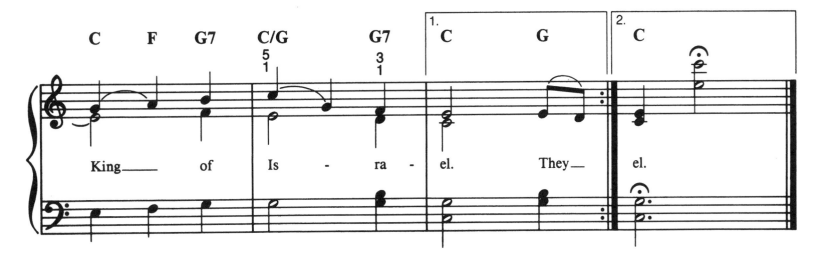

THE FRIENDLY BEASTS

Traditional English Carol

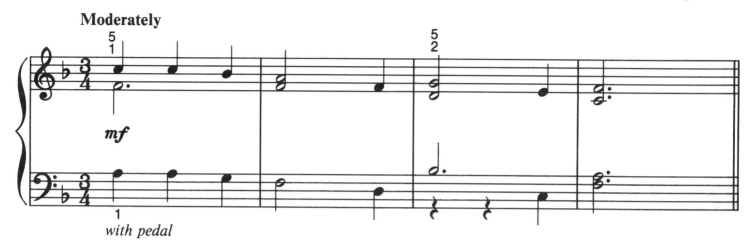

Moderately

mf

with pedal

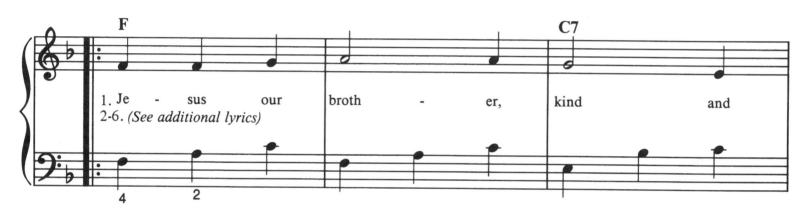

F

1. Je - sus our broth - er, kind and
2-6. *(See additional lyrics)*

C7

F

good Was hum - bly born in a

Bb

C7

sta - ble rude, And the friend - ly beasts a -

F **Bb** **F**

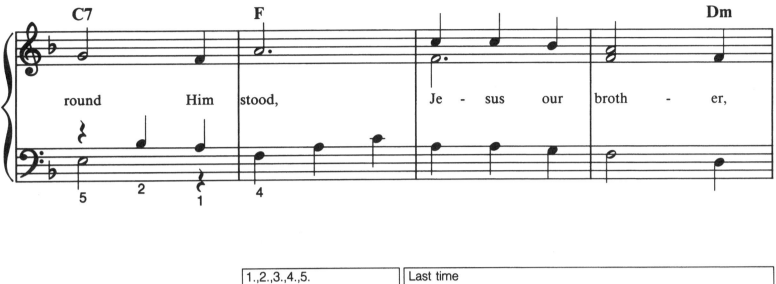

round Him stood, Je - sus our broth - er,

kind and good.

2. "I," said the donkey, shaggy and brown,
   "I carried His mother up hill and down;
   I carried her safely to Bethlehem town."
   "I," said the donkey, shaggy and brown.

3. "I," said the cow all white and red,
   "I gave Him my manger for His bed;
   I gave Him my hay to pillow his head."
   "I," said the cow all white and red.

4. "I," said the sheep with curly horn,
   "I gave Him my wool for His blanket warm;
   He wore my coat on Christmas morn."
   "I," said the sheep with curly horn.

5. "I," said the dove from the rafters high,
   "I cooed Him to sleep so He would not cry,
   We cooed Him to sleep, my mate and I."
   "I," said the dove from the rafter high.

6. Thus every beast by some good spell,
   In the stable dark was glad to tell
   Of the gift he gave Emanuel,
   The gift he gave Emanuel.

FROSTY THE SNOW MAN

Words and Music by STEVE NELSON
and JACK ROLLINS

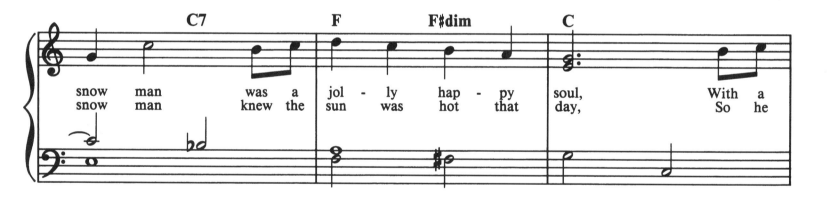

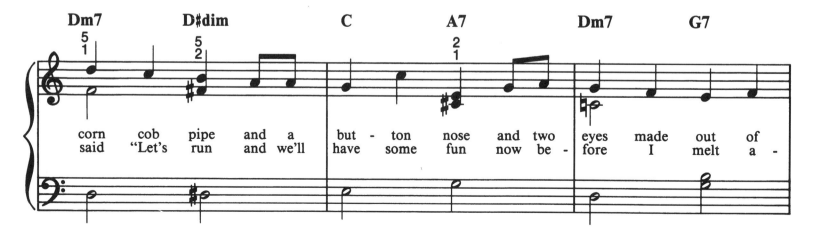

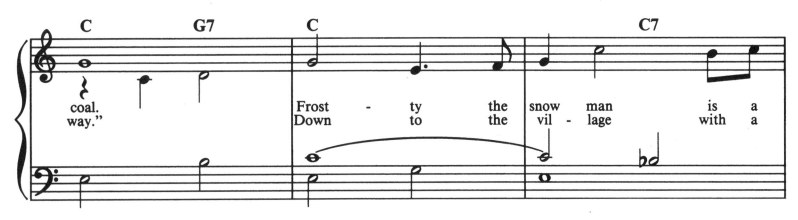

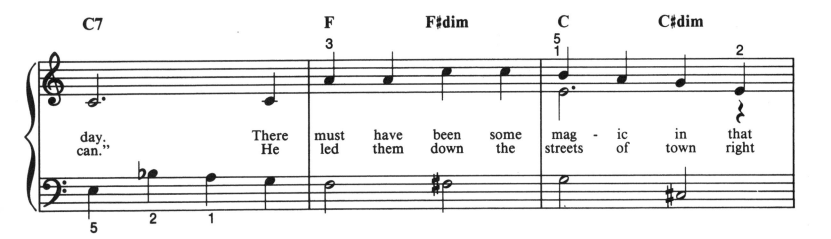

34

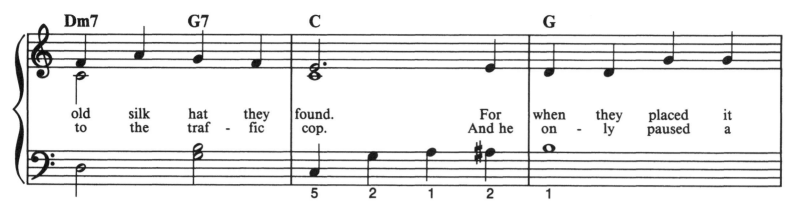

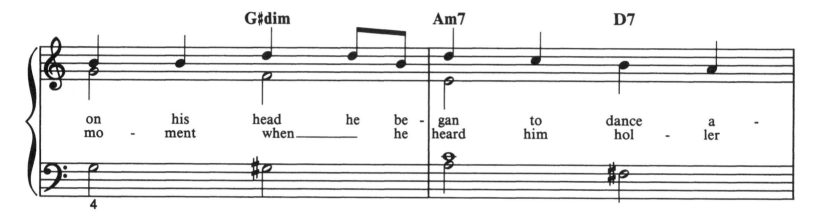

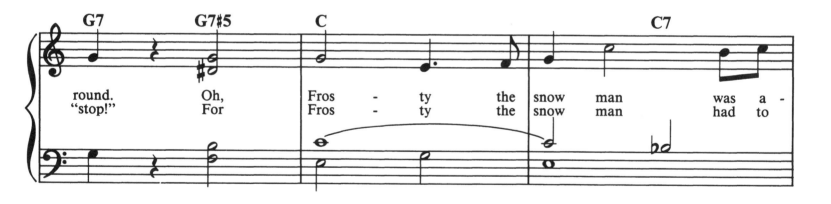

35

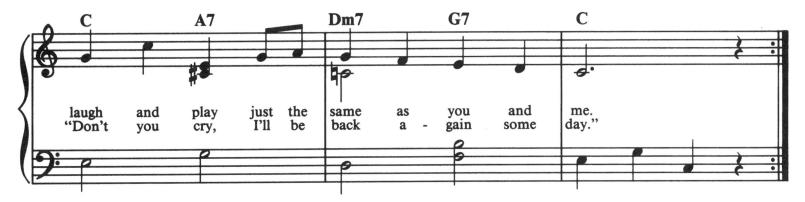

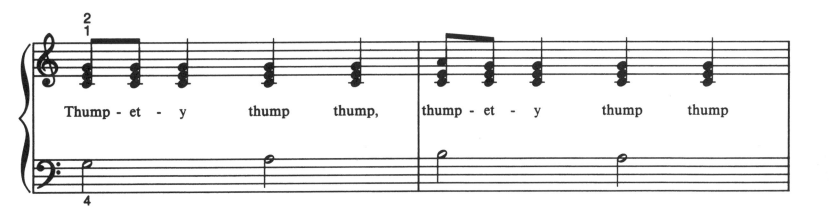

GO, TELL IT ON THE MOUNTAIN

African-American Spiritual
Verses by JOHN W. WORK, JR.

Moderately

with pedal

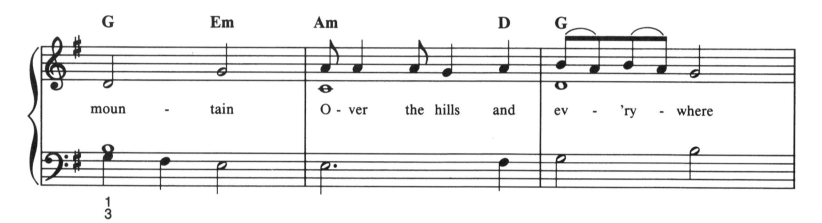

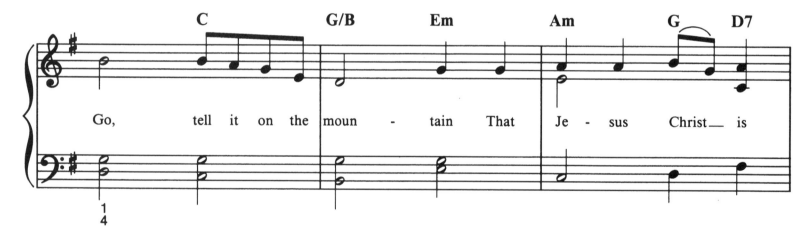

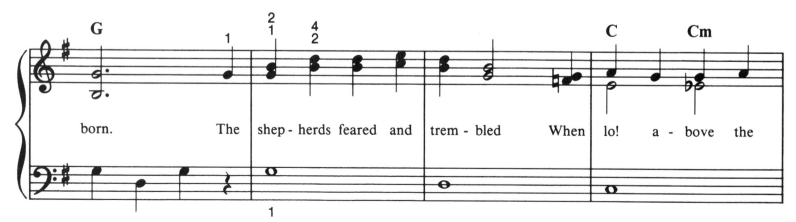

37

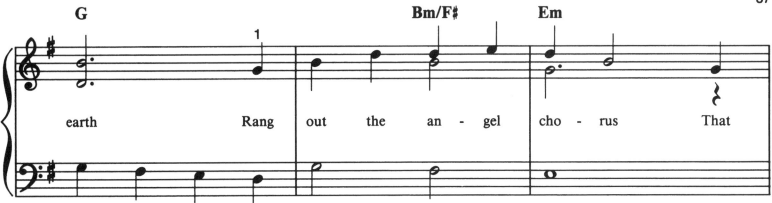

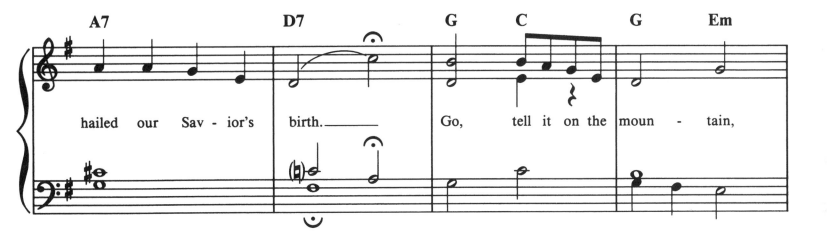

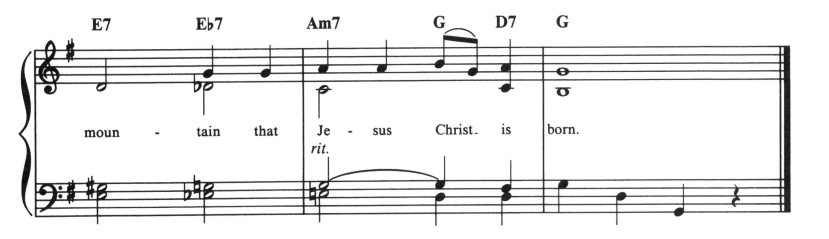

GOD REST YE MERRY, GENTLEMEN

19th Century English Carol

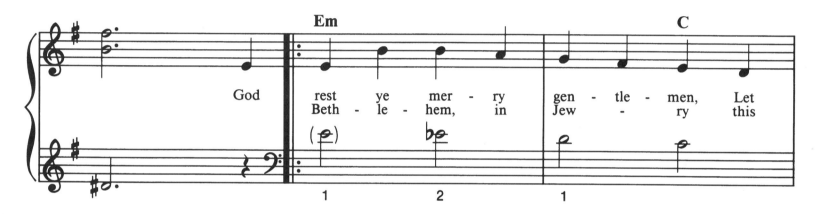

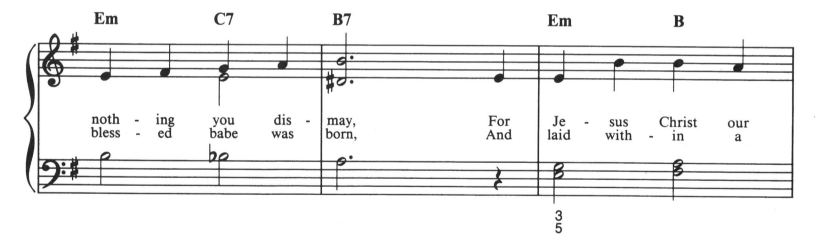

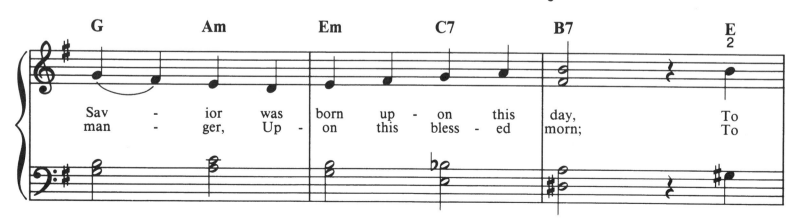

39

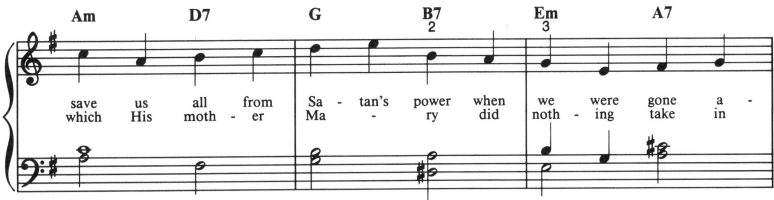

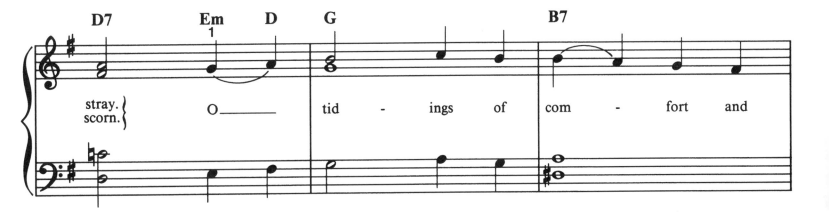

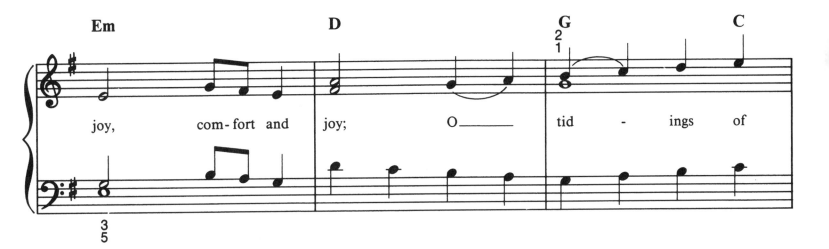

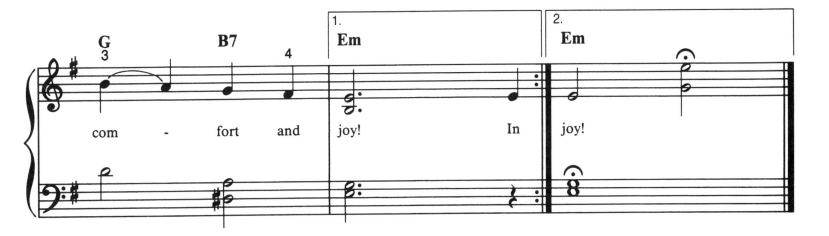

GOIN' ON A SLEIGHRIDE

Words and Music by
RALPH BLANE

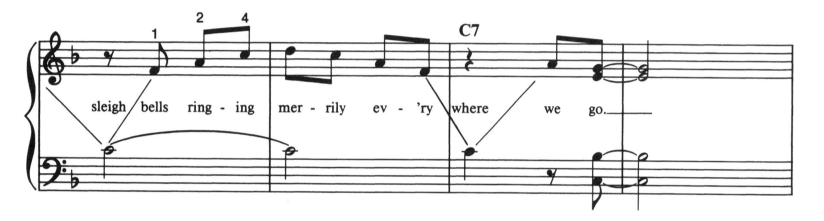

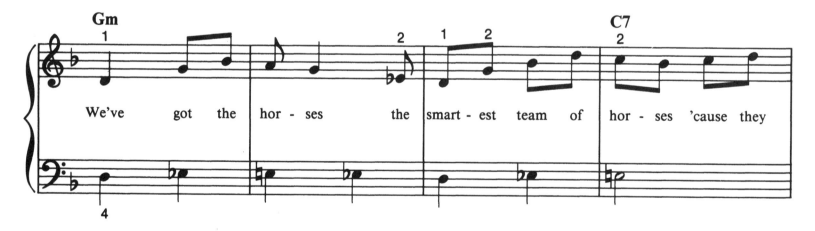

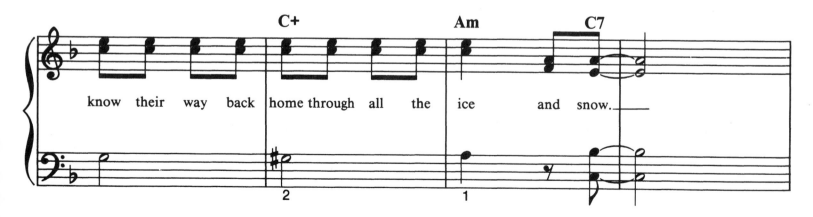

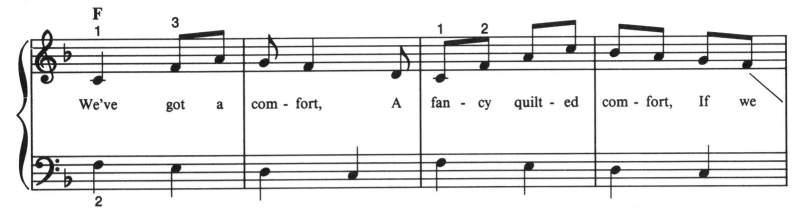

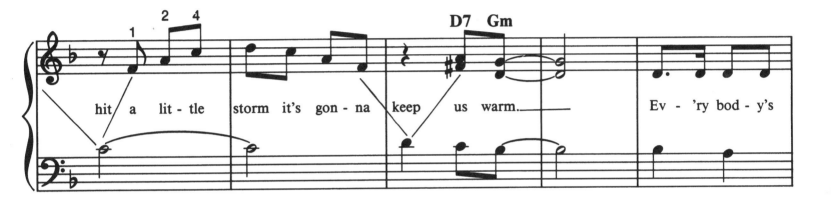

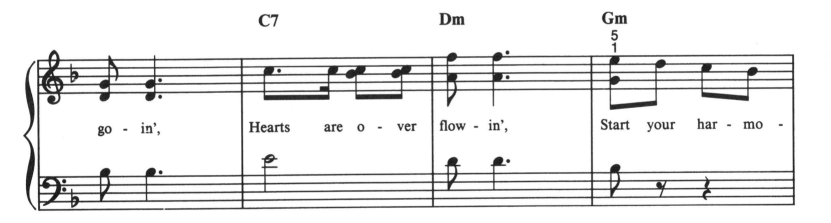

A little slower

Why don't you come a - long? We're go - in' on a sleigh ride,

mp

With Pedal

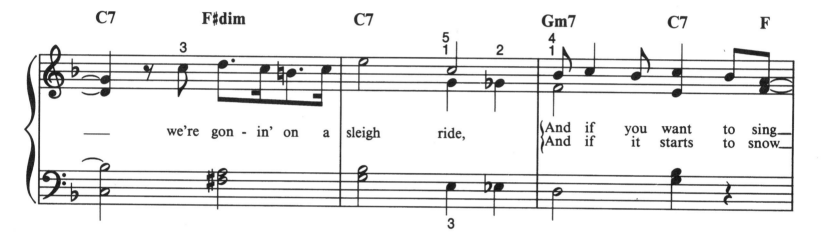

___ we're gon - in' on a sleigh ride, (And if you want to sing ___
(And if it starts to snow ___

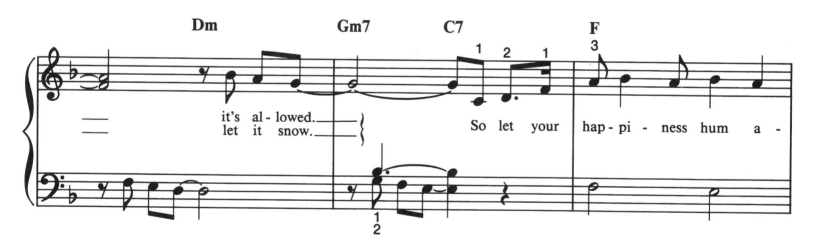

___ it's al - lowed. ___ So let your hap - pi - ness hum a -
let it snow. ___

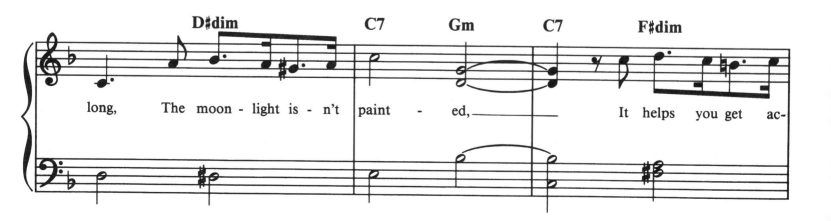

long, The moon - light is - n't paint - ed, ___ It helps you get ac-

quaint - ed

And starts you pair - in' off _____ from the crowd _____
You'll steal a kiss with - out _____ mis - tle - toe _____

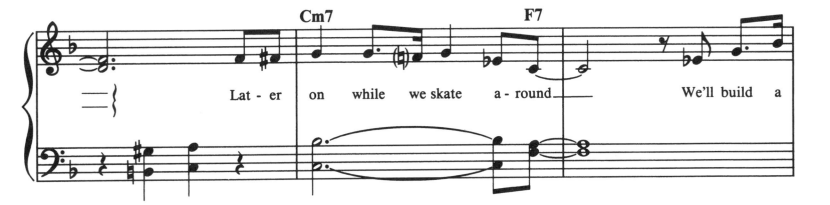

Lat - er on while we skate a - round _____ We'll build a

fire and we'll wait a-round _____ Un - til a co - zy cor - ner can be found. _____

Then what-'ll we do? I'll leave it to you, ___ We're gon - na

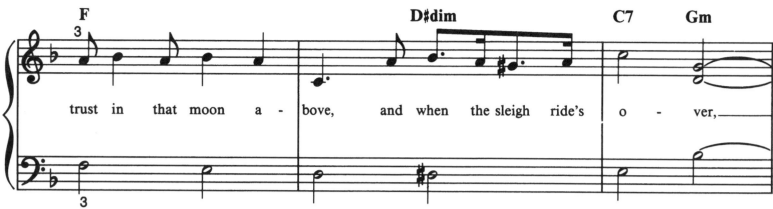

trust in that moon a - bove, and when the sleigh ride's o - ver,

we're gon - na be in clo - ver, af - ter we cud - dle

near, May - be we'll find that we're

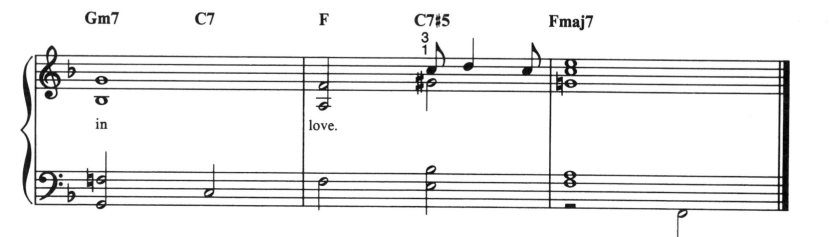

in love.

A HOLLY JOLLY CHRISTMAS

Music and Lyrics by
JOHNNY MARKS

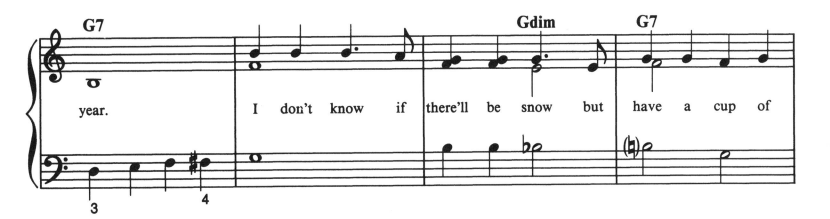

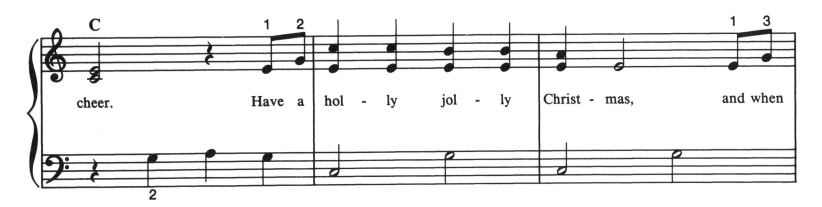

46

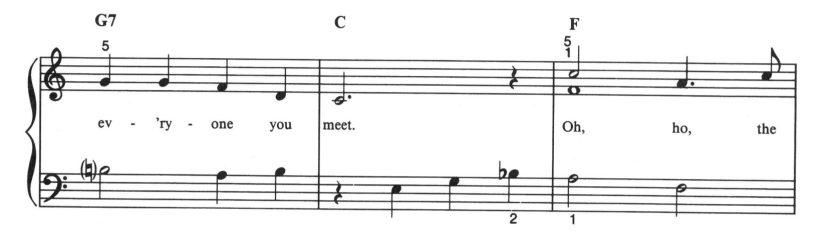

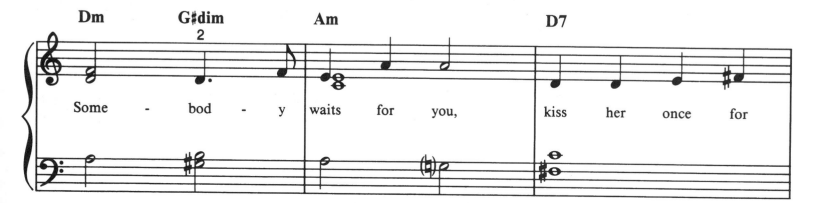

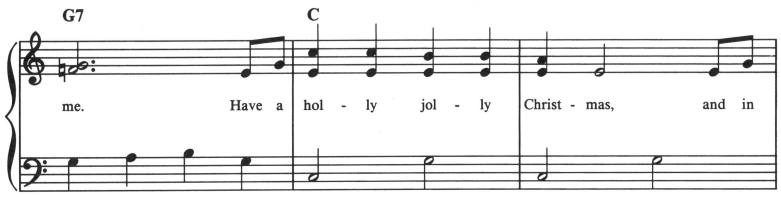

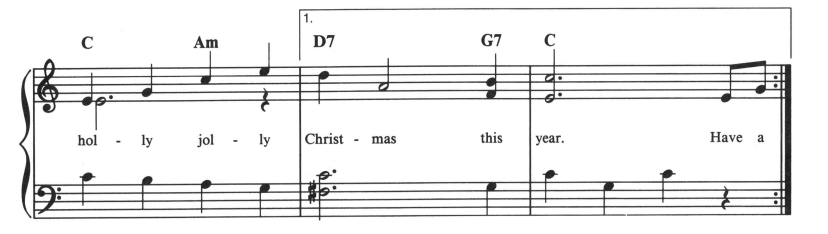

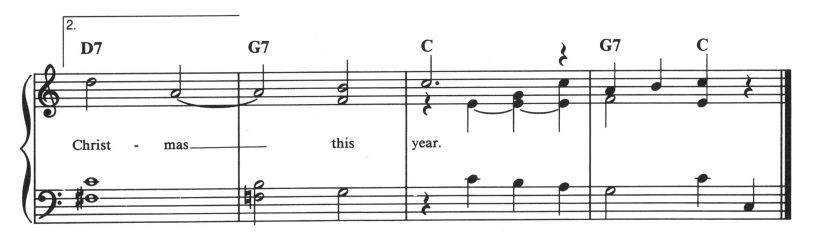

GOOD CHRISTIAN MEN, REJOICE

14th Century Latin Text
Translated by JOHN MASON NEALE
14th Century German Melody

With spirit

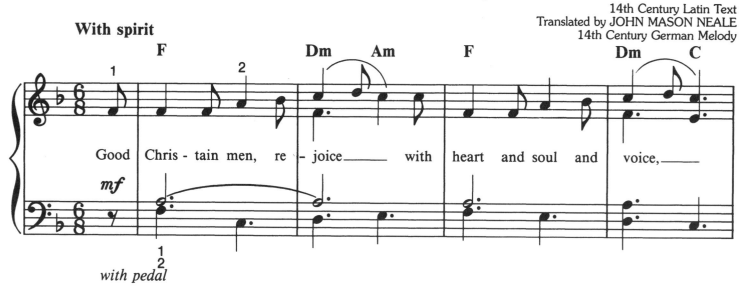

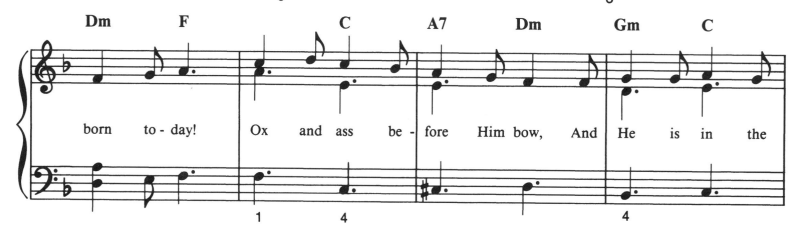

Chris - tian men, re - joice_____ with heart and soul and voice_____

Now ye hear of end - less bliss; Joy! Joy! Je - sus Christ was

born for this. He hath ope'd the heav'n - ly door, And man is bless - ed

ev - er - more. Christ was born for this!_____ Christ was born for this!

GOOD KING WENCESLAS

With spirit

Words by JOHN M. NEALE
Music from *Piae Cantiones*

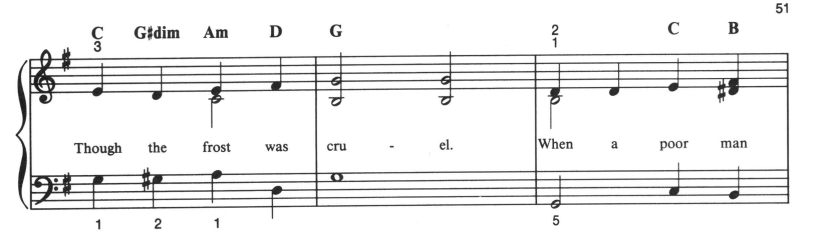

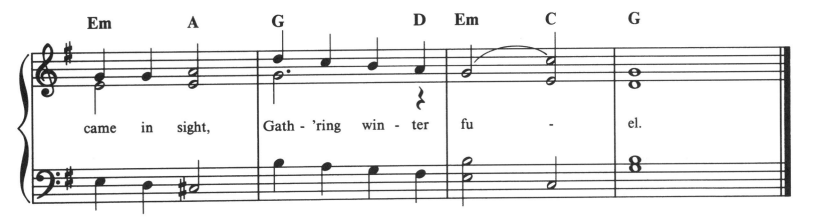

2.
"Hither page, and stand by me,
   If thou know'st it, telling,
Yonder peasant, who is he?
   Where and what his dwelling?"
"Sire, he lives a good league hence,
   Underneath the mountain;
Right against the forest fence,
   By Saint Agnes' fountain."

3.
"Bring me flesh, and bring me wine,
   Bring me pine-logs hither;
Thou and I will see him dine,
   When we bear them thither."
Page and monarch forth they went,
   Forth they went together;
Through the rude winds wild lament:
   And the bitter weather.

4.
"Sire, the night is darker now,
   And the wind blows stronger;
Fails my heart, I know not how,
   I can go not longer."
"Mark my footsteps, my good page,
   Tread thou in them boldly:
Thou shalt find the winter's rage
   Freeze thy blood less coldly."

5.
In his master's steps he trod,
   Where the snow lay dinted;
Heat was in the very sod
   Which the saint had printed.
Therefore, Christian men, be sure,
   Wealth or rank possessing,
Ye who now will bless the poor,
   Shall yourselves find blessing.

HARK! THE HERALD ANGELS SING

Words by CHARLES WESLEY
Altered by GEORGE WHITEFIELD
Music by FELIX MENDELSSOHN-BARTHOLDY

Moderately

with pedal

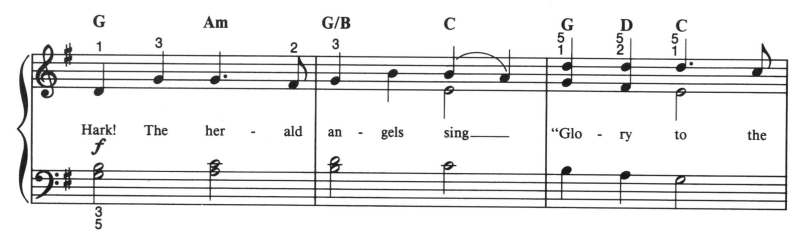

Hark! The her - ald an - gels sing—— "Glo - ry to the

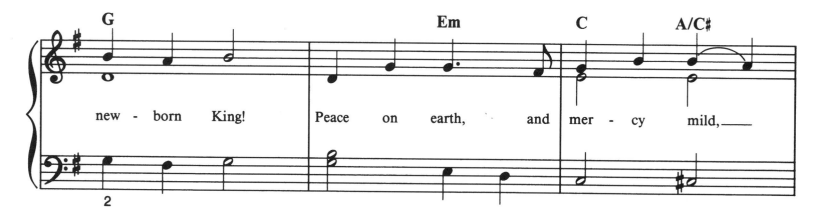

new - born King! Peace on earth, and mer - cy mild,——

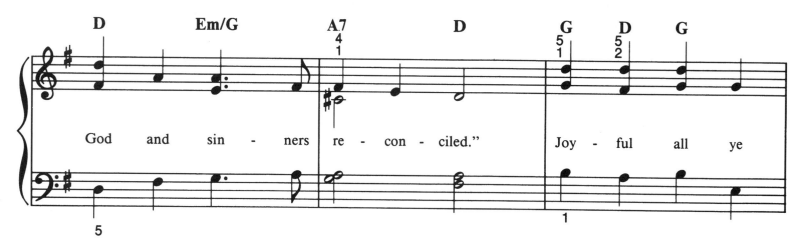

God and sin - ners re - con - ciled." Joy - ful all ye

53

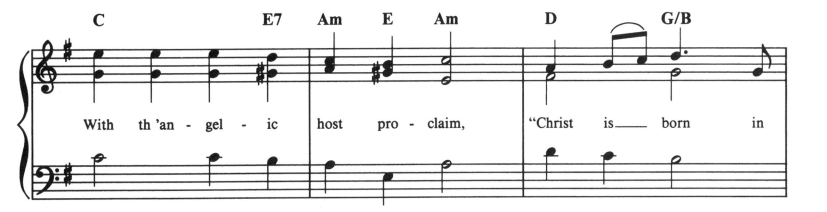

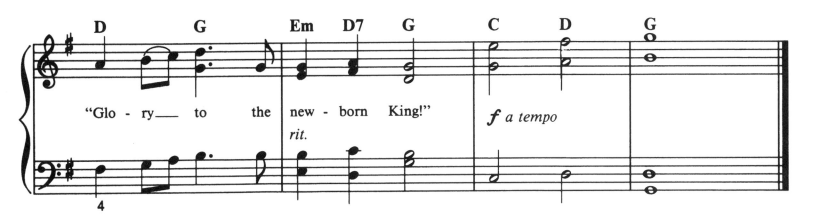

HERE WE COME A-WASSAILING

Traditional

Here we come a-was-sail-ing A-
We're not dai-ly beg-gars that

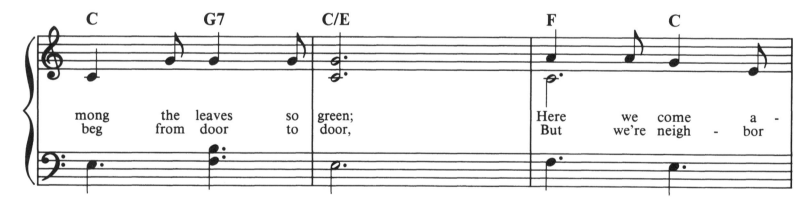

mong the leaves so green; Here we come a-
beg from door to door, But we're neigh-bor

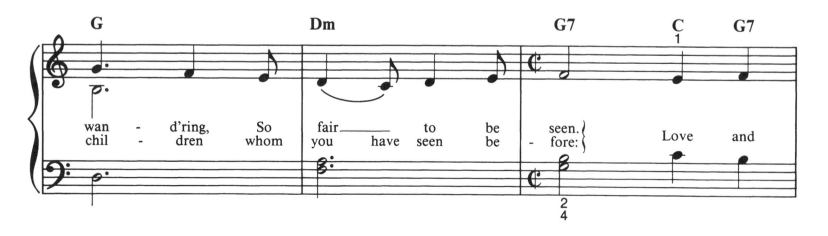

wan - d'ring, So fair to be seen. Love and
chil - dren whom you have seen be - fore:

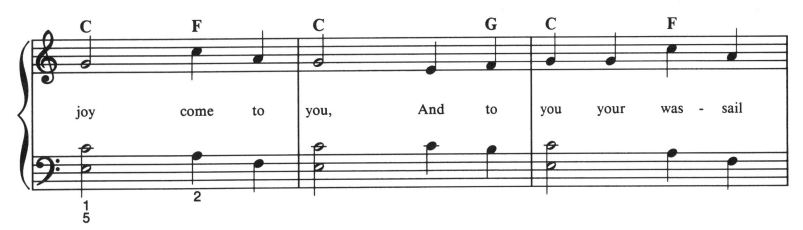

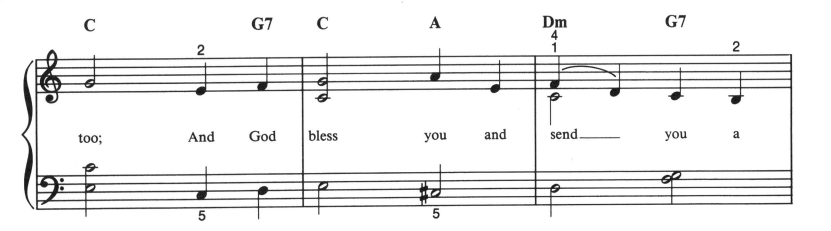

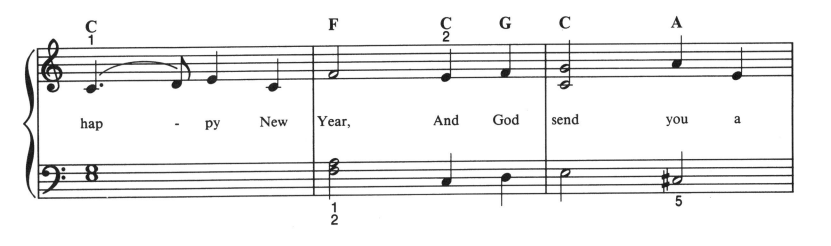

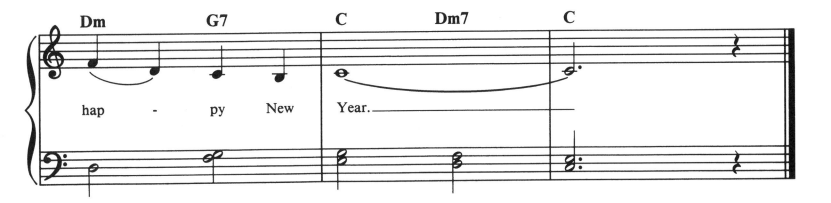

(There's No Place Like)
HOME FOR THE HOLIDAYS

Words by AL STILLMAN
Music by ROBERT ALLEN

Moderately

mf

Oh, there's

With Pedal

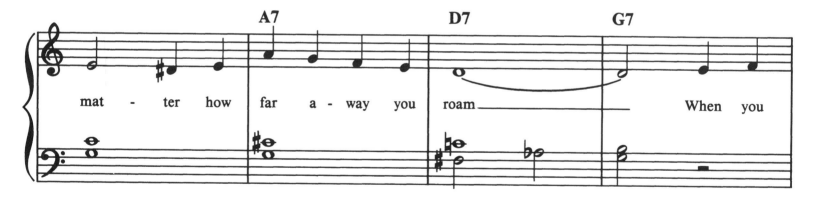

C   C7   F   C

no   place   like   home   for   the   hol - i - days____   'cause   no

A7   D7   G7

mat - ter   how   far   a - way   you   roam____   When   you

C   C7   F   F#dim   C

pine   for   the   sun - shine   of   a   friend - ly   gaze____

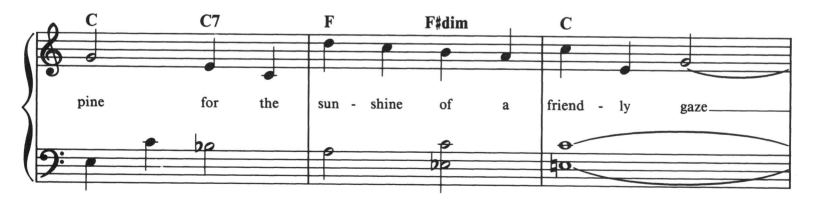

for the hol - i - days you can't beat home, sweet home.

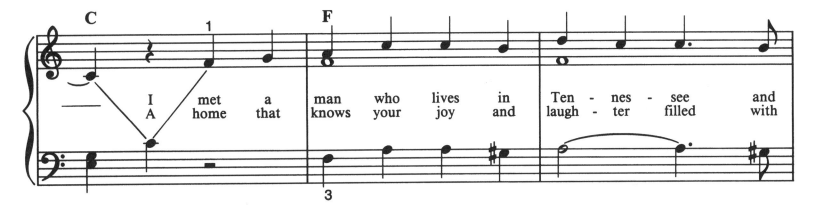

I met a man who lives in Ten - nes - see and
A home that knows your joy and laugh - ter filled with

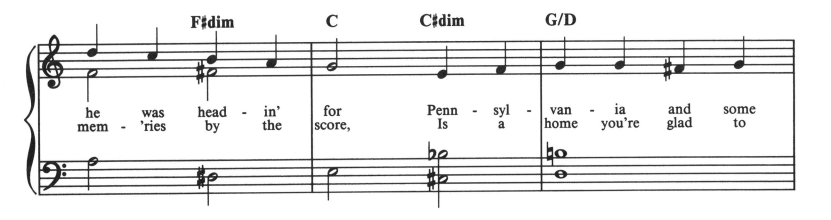

he was head - in' for Penn - syl - van - ia and some
mem - 'ries by the score, Is a home you're glad to

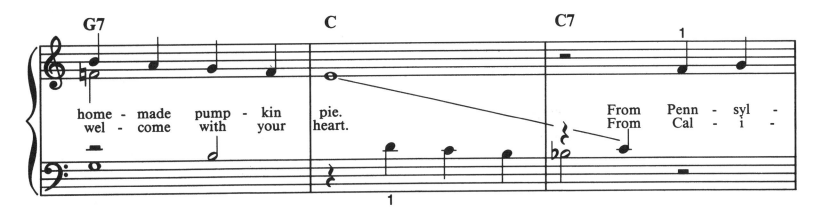

home - made pump - kin pie. From Penn - syl -
wel - come with your heart. From Cal - i -

58

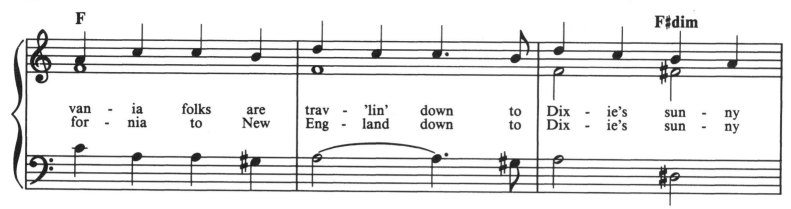

F   F#dim

van - ia   folks   are   trav - 'lin'   down   to   Dix - ie's   sun - ny
for - nia   to   New   Eng - land   down   to   Dix - ie's   sun - ny

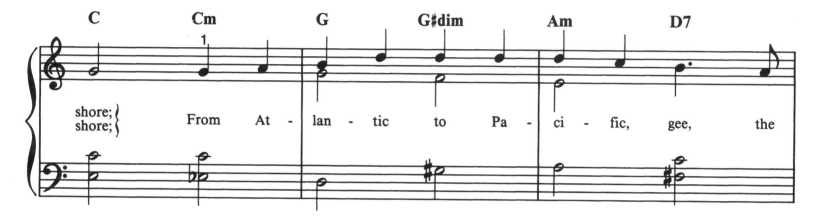

C   Cm   G   G#dim   Am   D7

shore;
shore;   From   At - lan - tic   to   Pa - ci - fic,   gee,   the

G7   Gdim   G7   C   C7

traf - fic   is   ter - ri - fic.   Oh,   there's   no   place   like

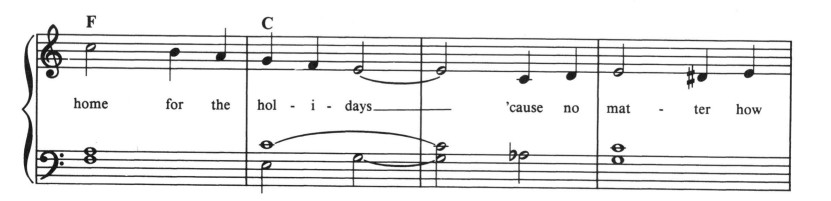

F   C

home   for   the   hol - i - days_____   'cause   no   mat - ter   how

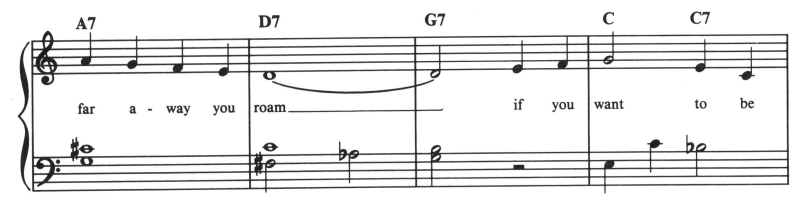

far a - way you roam _____ if you want to be

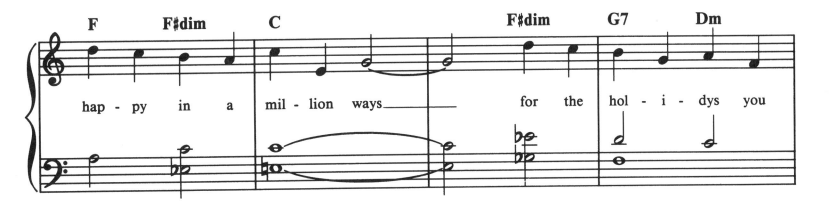

hap - py in a mil - lion ways _____ for the hol - i - dys you

1.
can't beat home sweet home. Oh, there's

2.
can't beat

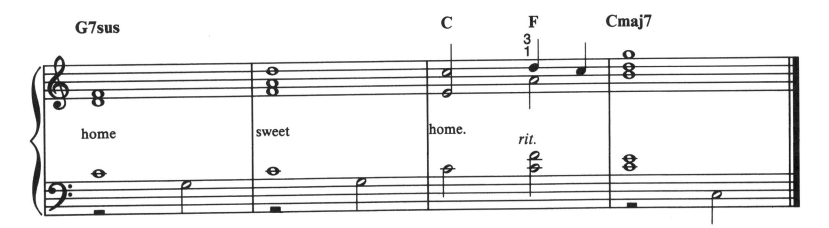

home sweet home. *rit.*

I HEARD THE BELLS ON CHRISTMAS DAY

Words by HENRY WADSWORTH LONGFELLOW
Music by JOHN BAPTISTE CALKIN

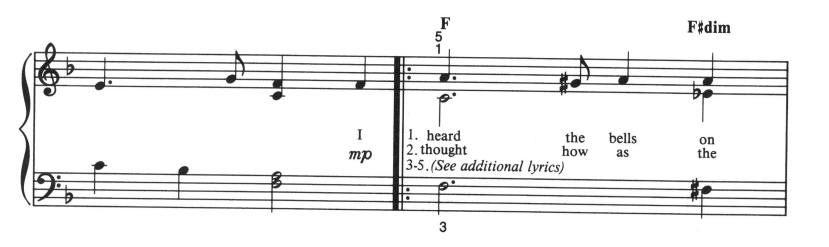

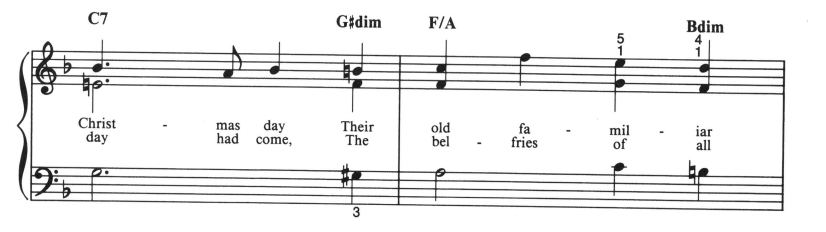

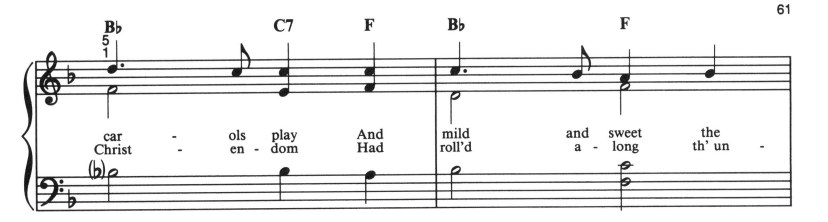

car - ols play And
Christ - en - dom And Had

mild and sweet the
roll'd a - long th' un -

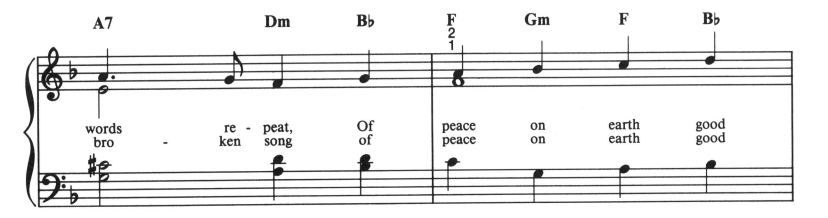

words re - peat, Of
bro - ken song Of

peace on earth good
peace on earth good

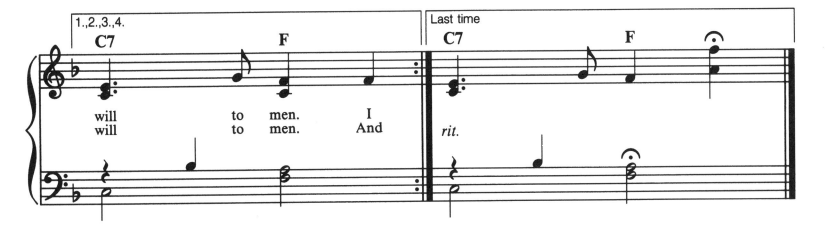

1.,2.,3.,4.

will to men. I
will to men. And

Last time

rit.

3. And in despair I bow'd my head:
   "There is no peace on earth," I said,
   "For hate is strong, and mocks the song
   Of peace on earth, good will to men."

4. Then pealed the bells more loud and deep:
   "God is not dead, nor doth He sleep;
   The wrong shall fail, the right prevail,
   With peace on earth, good will to men."

5. Till, ringing, singing on its way,
   The world revolved from night to day,
   A voice, a chime, a chant sublime,
   Of peace on earth, good will to men!

I SAW THREE SHIPS

Traditional

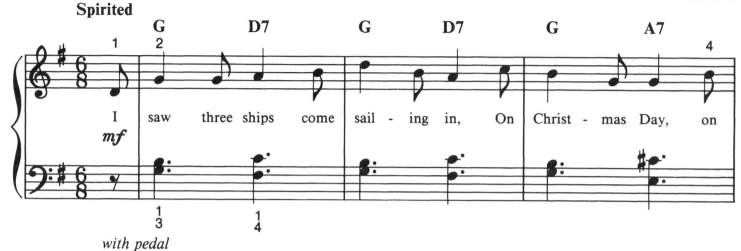

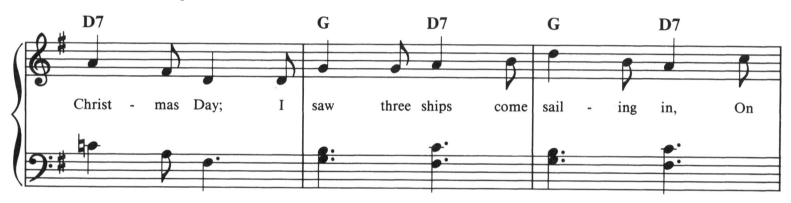

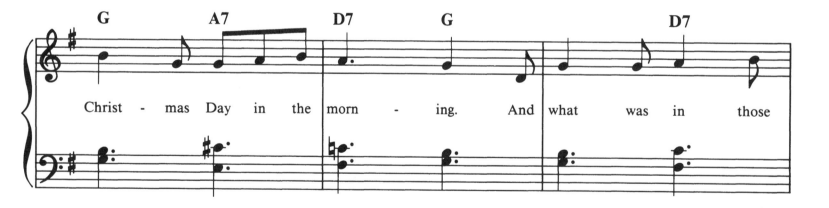

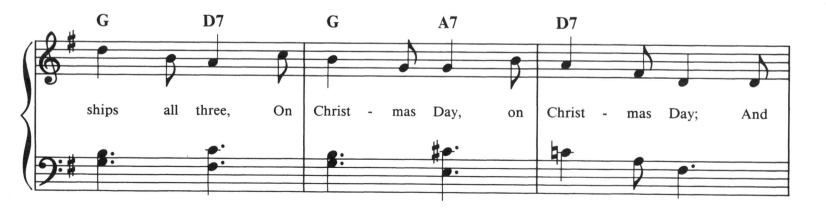

what was in those ships all three, On Christ-mas Day in the

morn - ing. The Vir - gin Mar - y and Christ were there, On

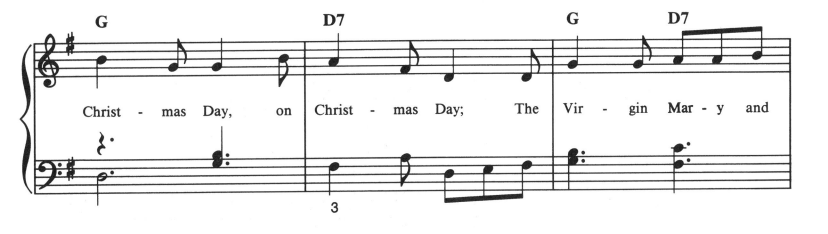

Christ - mas Day, on Christ - mas Day; The Vir - gin Mar - y and

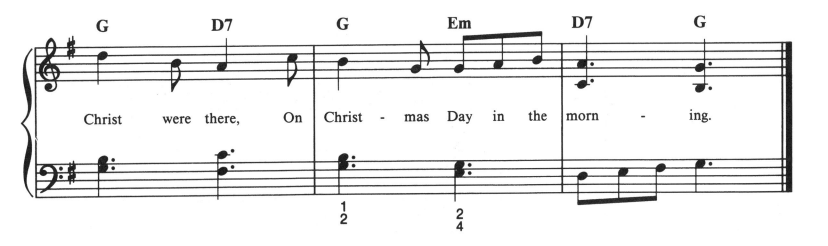

Christ were there, On Christ - mas Day in the morn - ing.

I'LL BE HOME FOR CHRISTMAS

Words and Music by KIM GANNON
and WALTER KENT

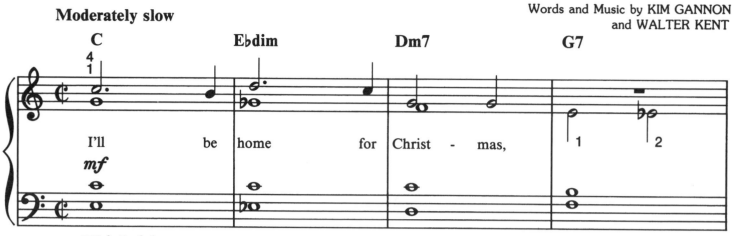

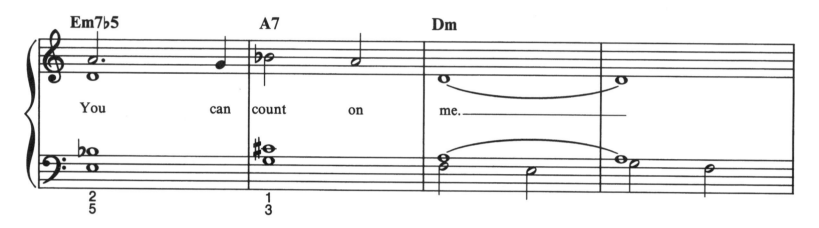

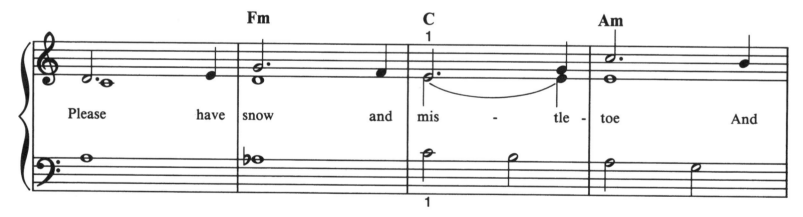

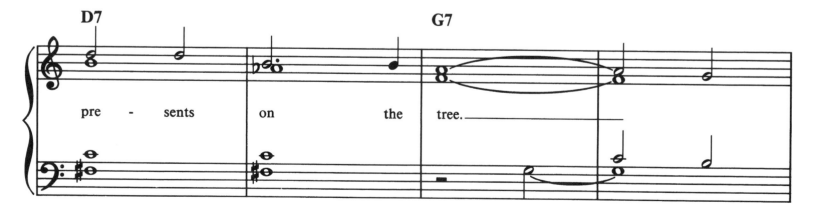

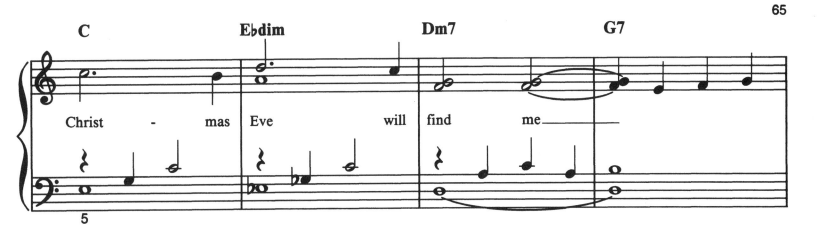

Christ - mas Eve will find me

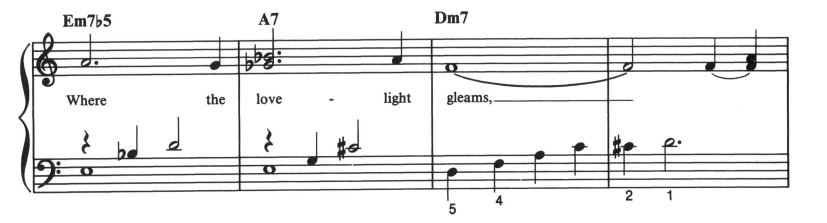

Where the love - light gleams,

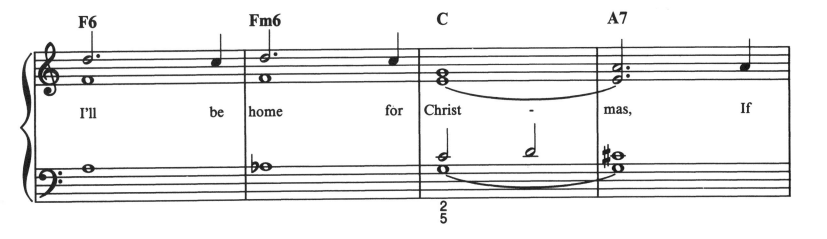

I'll be home for Christ - mas, If

on - ly in my dreams.
rit.

IT CAME UPON THE MIDNIGHT CLEAR

Words by EDMUND HAMILTON SEARS
Music by RICHARD STORRS WILLIS

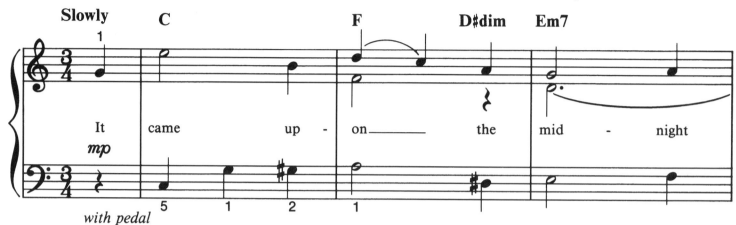

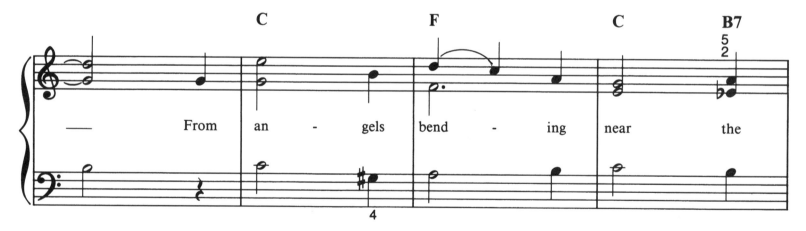

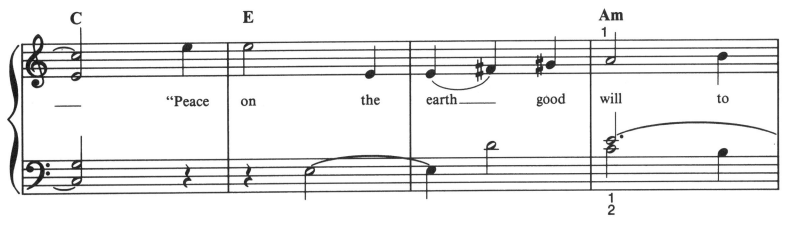

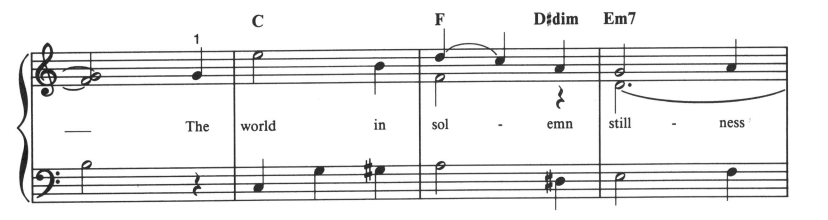

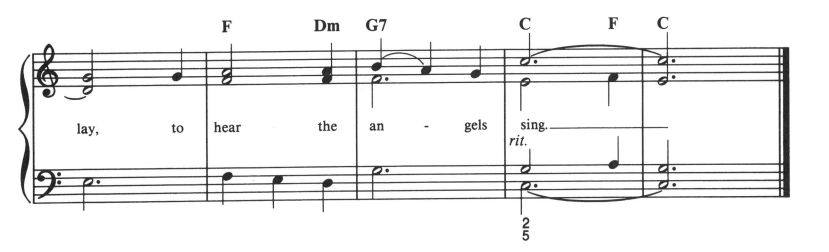

IT'S BEGINNING TO LOOK LIKE CHRISTMAS

By MEREDITH WILLSON

Moderately

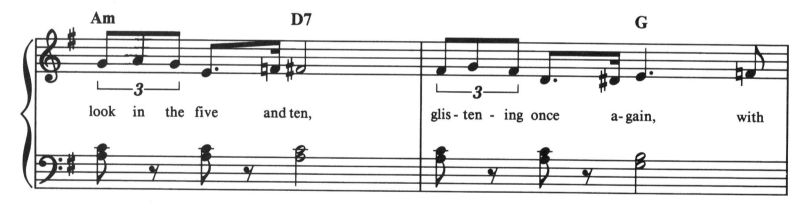

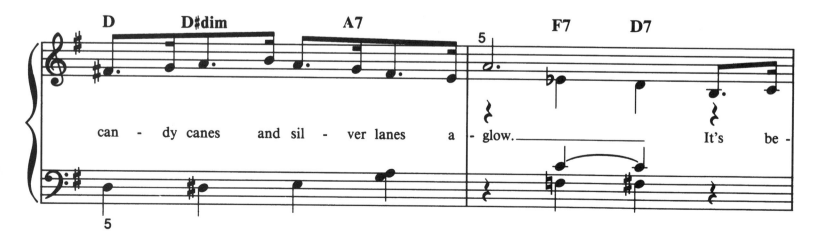

69

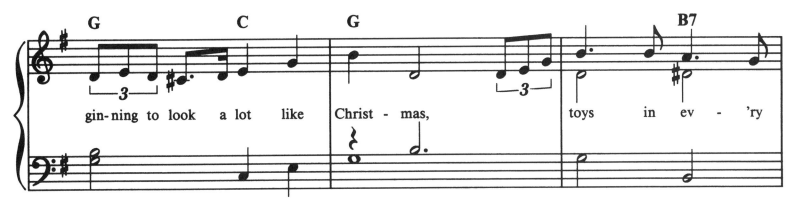

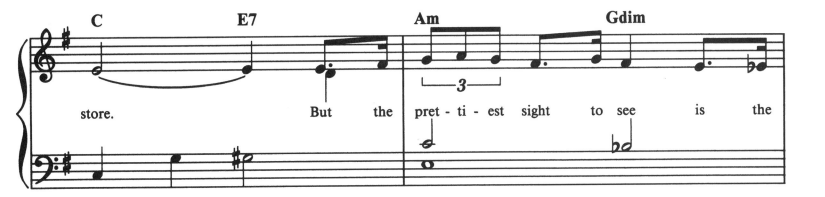

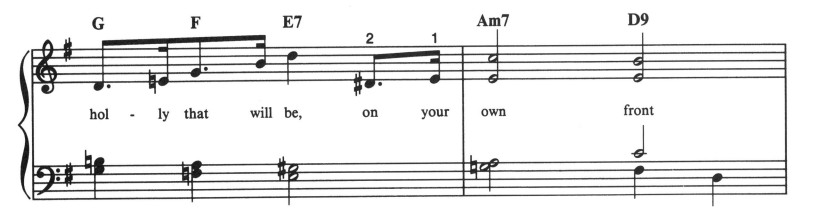

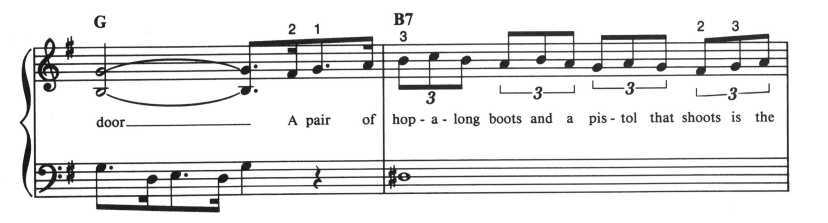

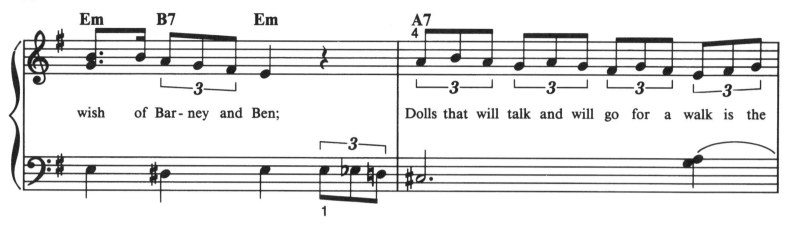

wish   of Bar-ney and Ben;   Dolls that will talk and will go for a walk is the

hope   of Jan-ice and Jen;   And Mom   and Dad   can hard-ly wait   for

school   to start a-gain.   It's be-gin-ning to look a lot   like   Christ-mas,

ev-'ry-where   you   go;___   There's a   tree in the Grand Ho-tel,

71

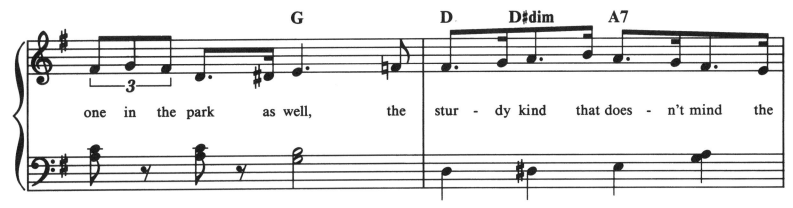

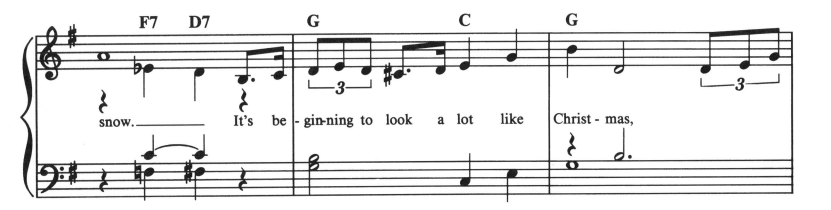

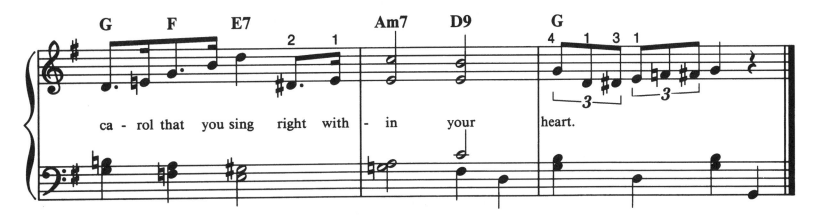

JINGLE-BELL ROCK

Words and Music by JOE BEAL
and JIM BOOTHE

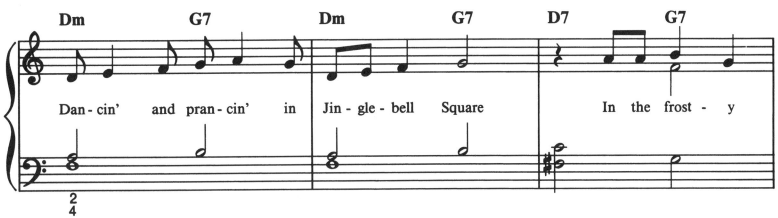

C   Em7♭5

Gid - dy - ap,   jin - gle horse   pick up your feet___   Jin - gle a - round the

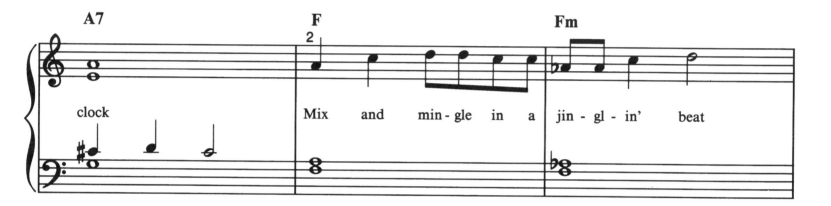

A7   F   Fm

clock   Mix   and   min - gle   in   a   jin - gl - in'   beat

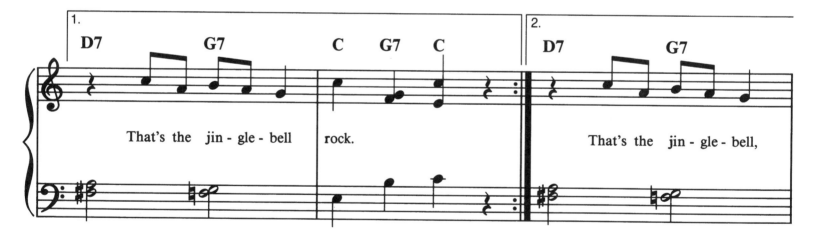

1.
D7   G7   C   G7   C   2.
                                             D7   G7

That's the jin - gle - bell   rock.   That's the jin - gle - bell,

D7   G7   D7   G7   C

That's the jin - gle- bell,   That's the jin - gle- bell   rock.

JINGLE, JINGLE, JINGLE

Music and Lyrics by
JOHNNY MARKS

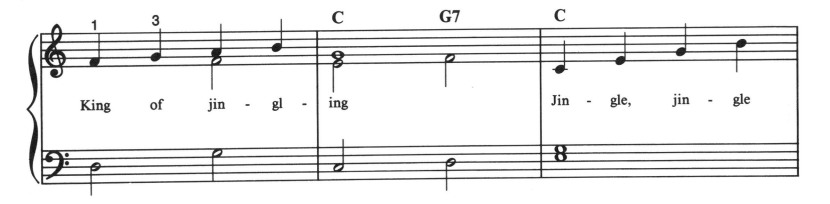

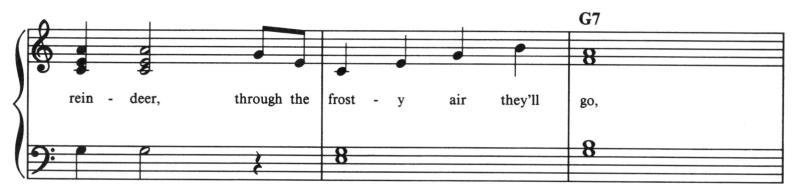

rein - deer, through the frost - y air they'll go,

They are not just plain deer, they're the fast - est deer I

know. You must be - lieve that on Christ - mas Eve

He won't pass you by, He'll dash a - way in his

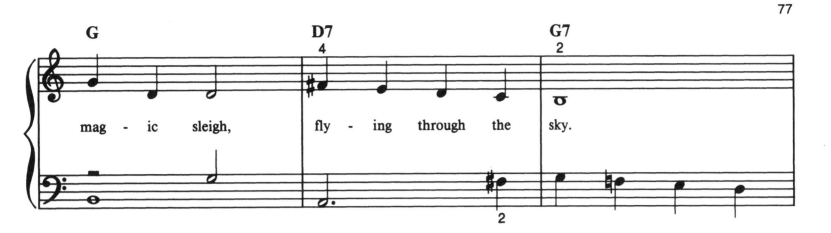

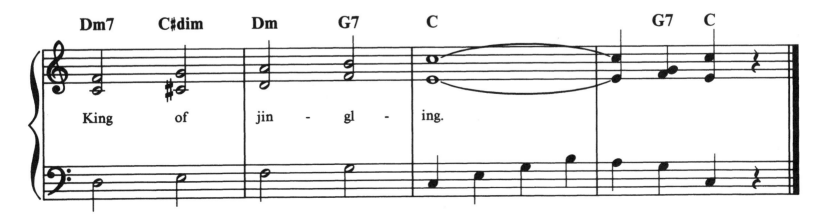

JINGLE BELLS

Words and Music by
J. PIERPONT

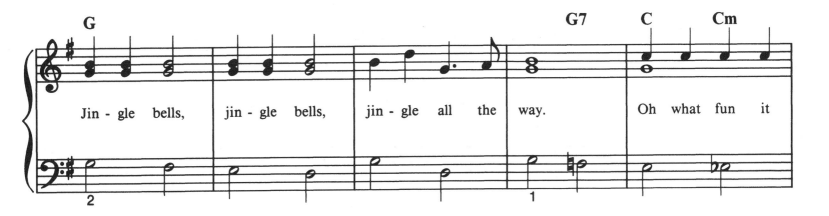

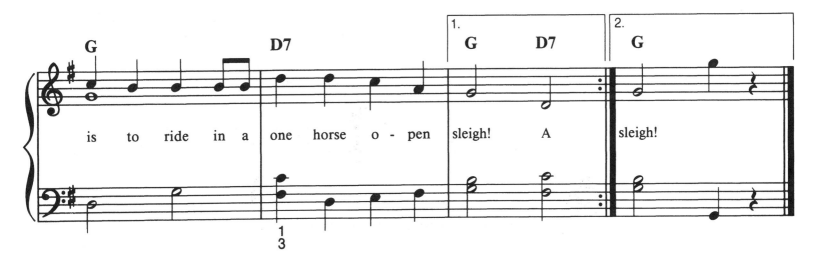

JOLLY OLD ST. NICHOLAS

Traditional 19th Century American Carol

Brightly

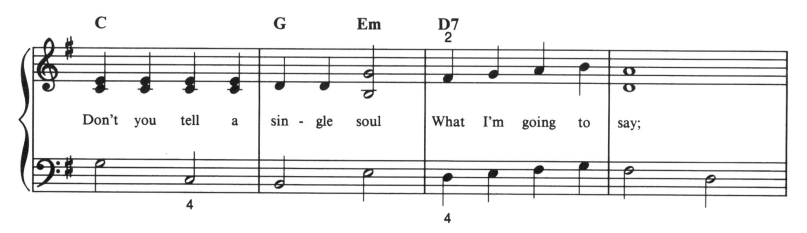

Jol - ly Old St. Ni - cho - las, Lean your ear this way!

mf

with pedal

Don't you tell a sin - gle soul What I'm going to say;

Christ - mas Eve is com - ing soon; Now you dear old man,

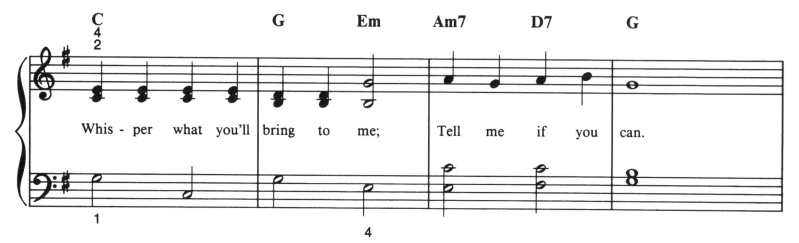

Whis - per what you'll bring to me; Tell me if you can.

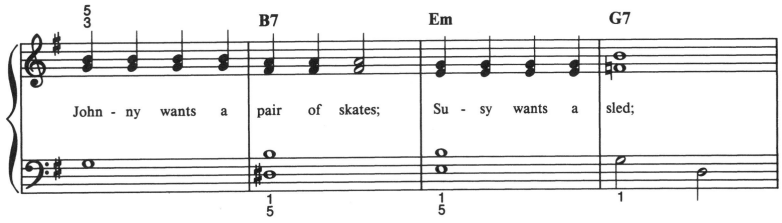

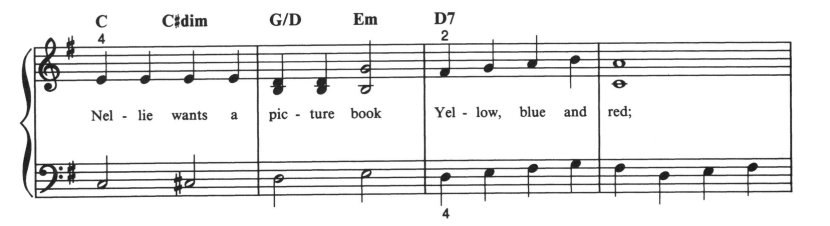

JOY TO THE WORLD

Words by ISAAC WATTS
Music by GEORGE FRIDERIC HANDEL

Moderately (in 2)

with pedal

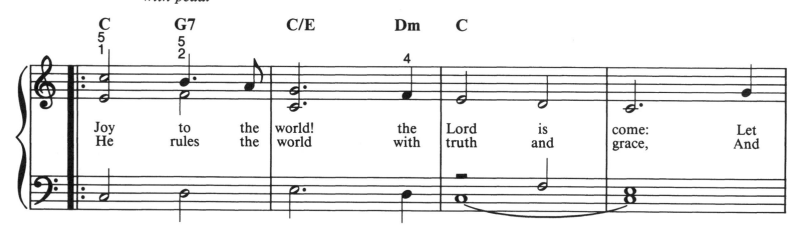

Joy to the world! the Lord is come: Let
He rules the world with truth and grace, And

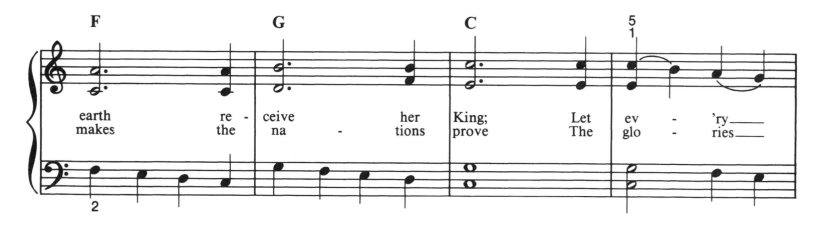

earth re-ceive her King; Let ev - 'ry
makes the na - tions prove The glo - ries

heart pre - pare Him room And
of His right - eous - ness, And

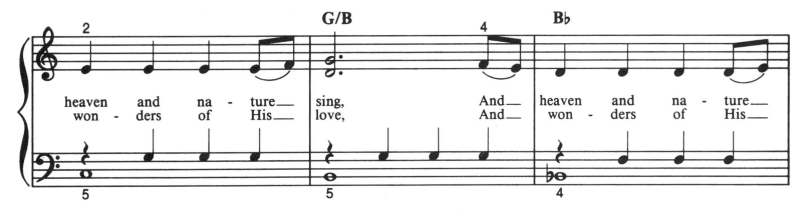

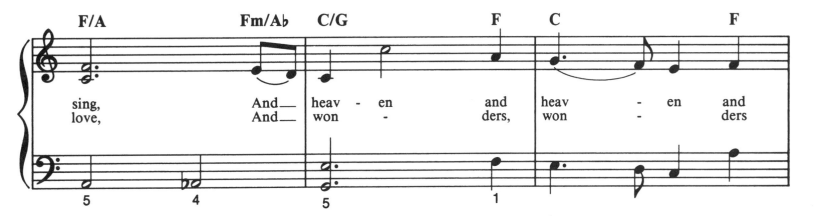

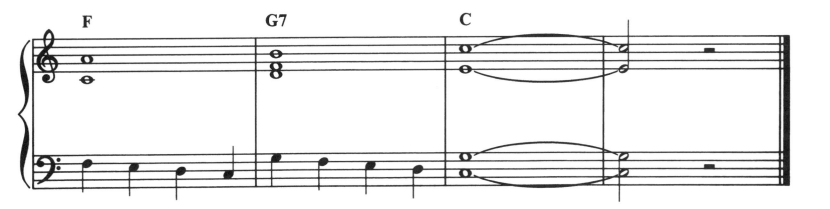

LET IT SNOW! LET IT SNOW! LET IT SNOW!

Words by SAMMY CAHN
Music by JULE STYNE

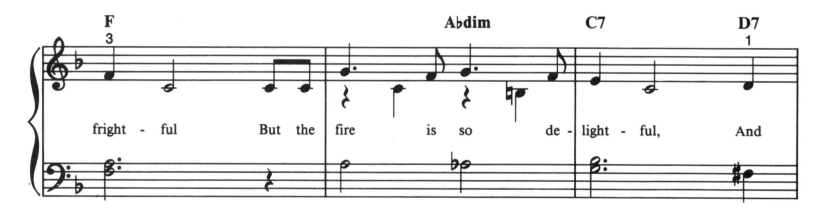

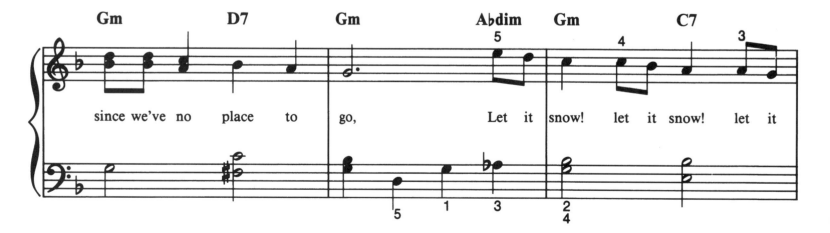

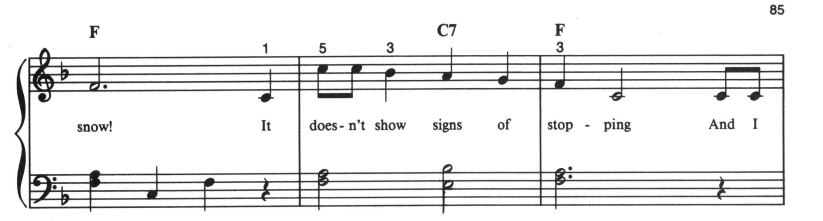

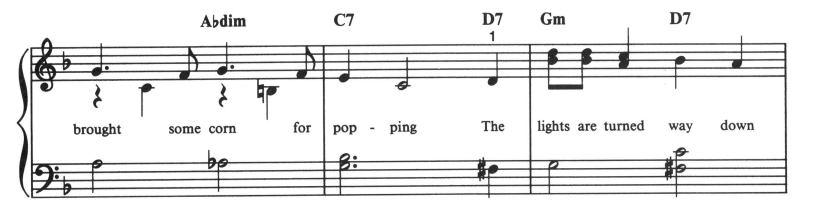

86

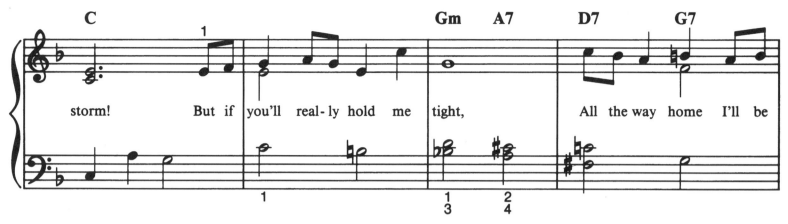

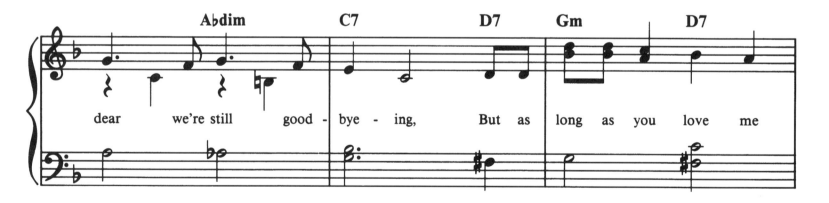

MARCH OF THE TOYS

By VICTOR HERBERT

Moderate March

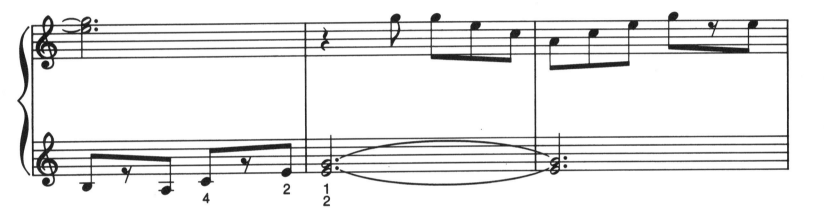

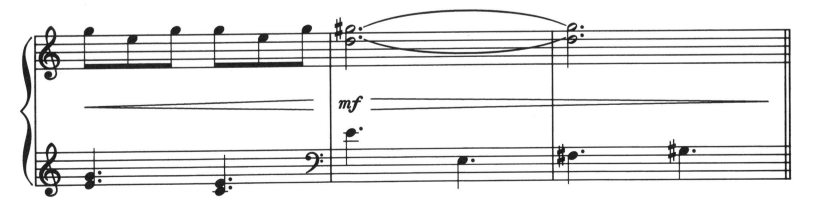

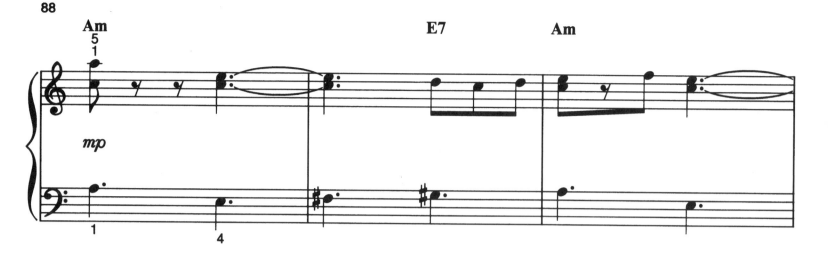

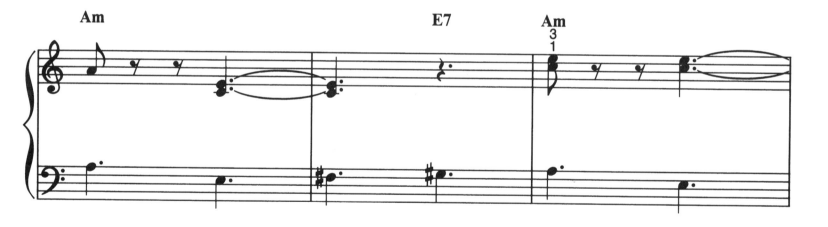

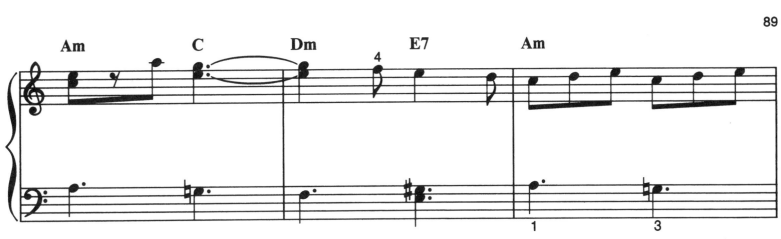

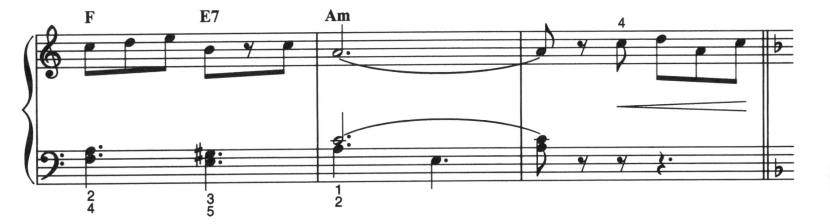

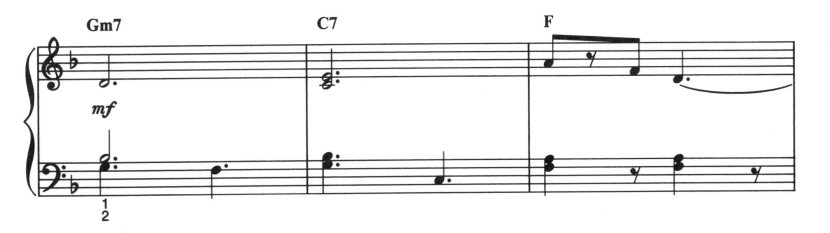

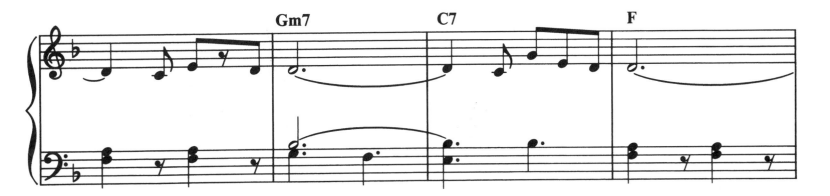

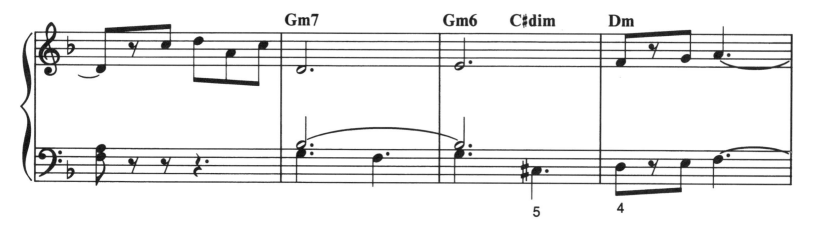

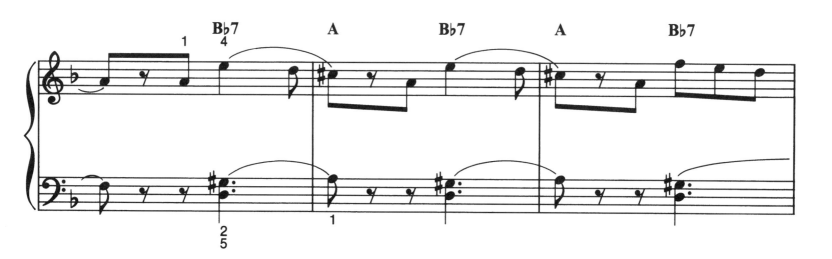

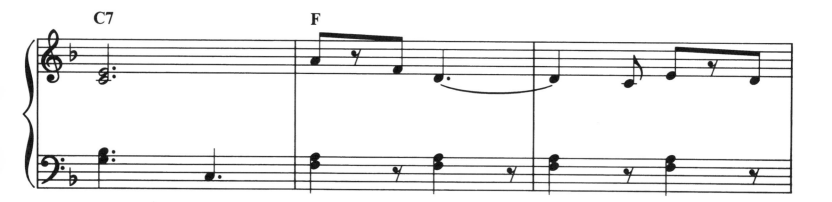

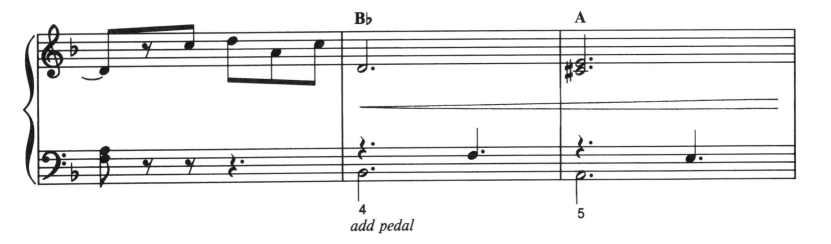

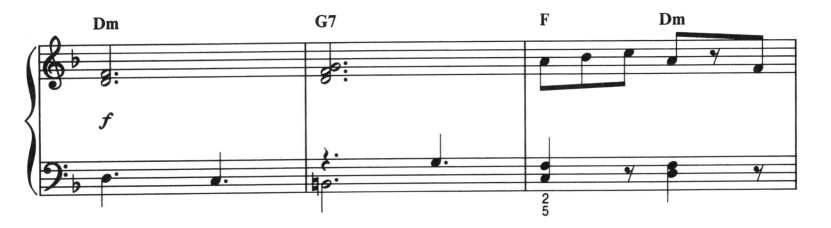

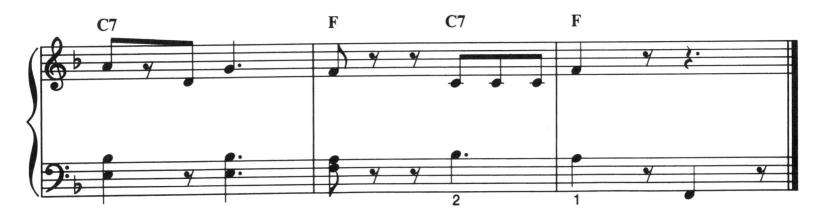

A MARSHMALLOW WORLD

Words by CARL SIGMAN
Music by PETER DE ROSE

Moderately

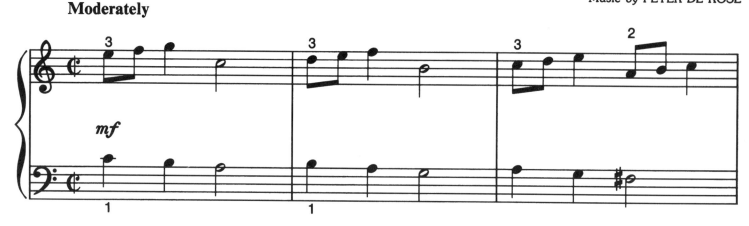

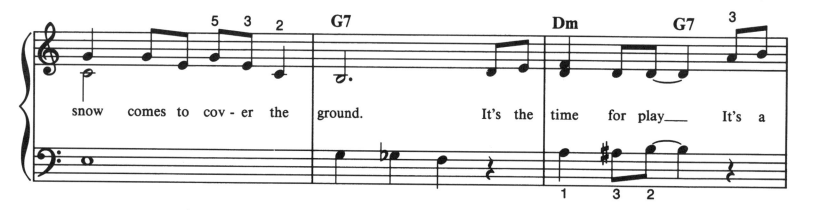

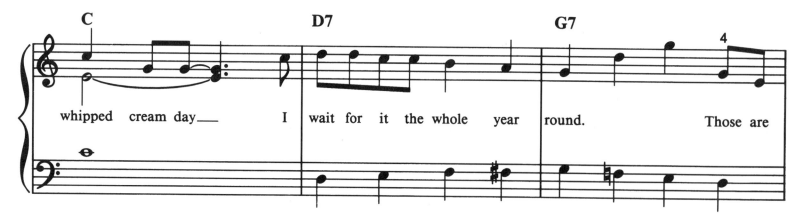

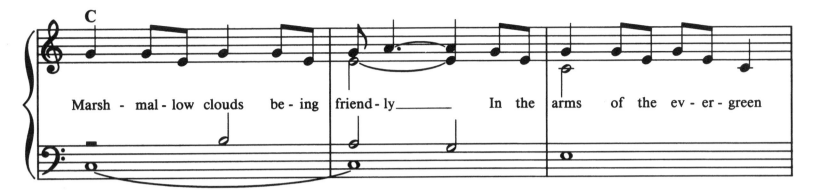

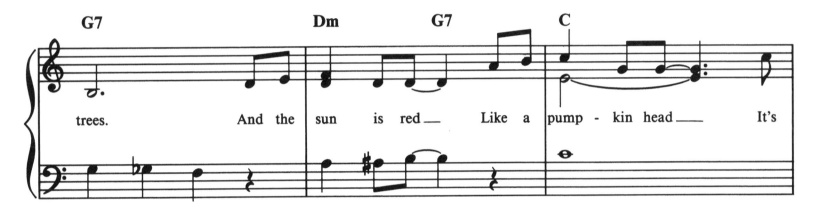

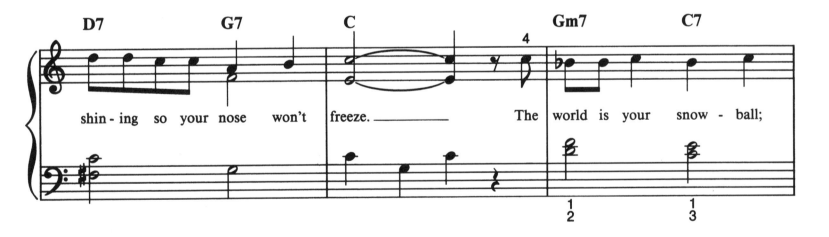

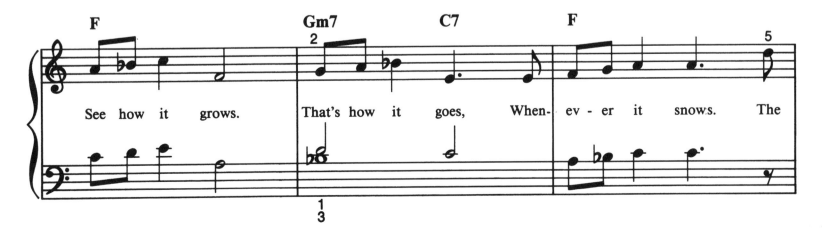

THE MERRY CHRISTMAS POLKA

Words by PAUL FRANCIS WEBSTER
Music by SONNY BURKE

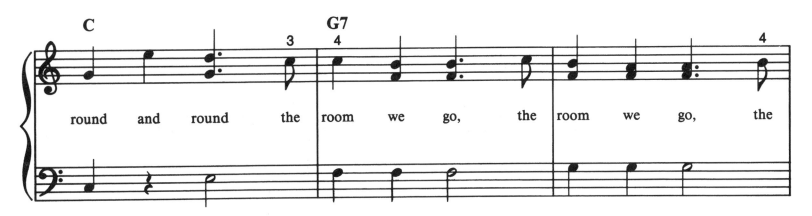

96

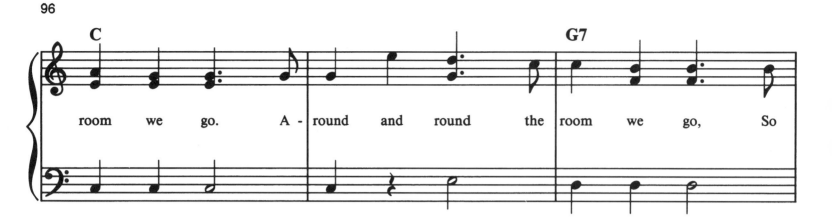

room we go. A - round and round the room we go, So

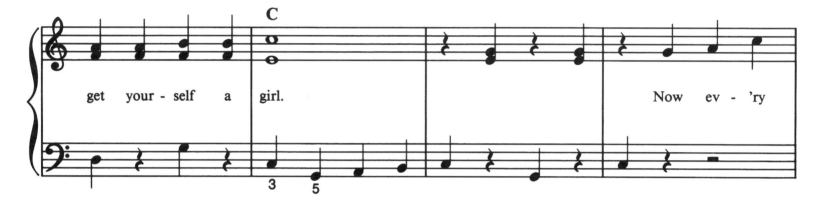

get your - self a girl. Now ev - 'ry

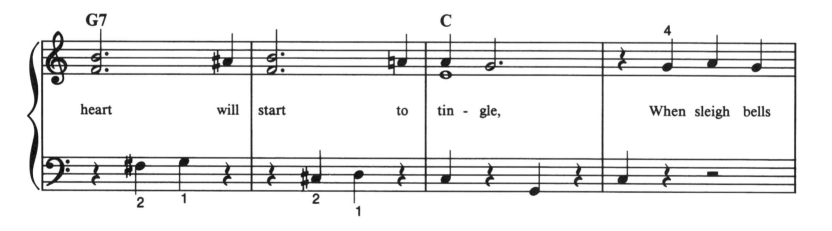

heart will start to tin - gle, When sleigh bells

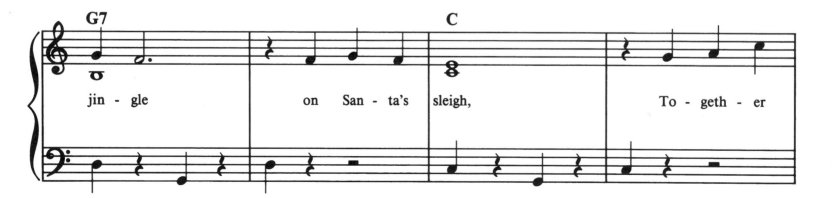

jin - gle on San - ta's sleigh, To - geth - er

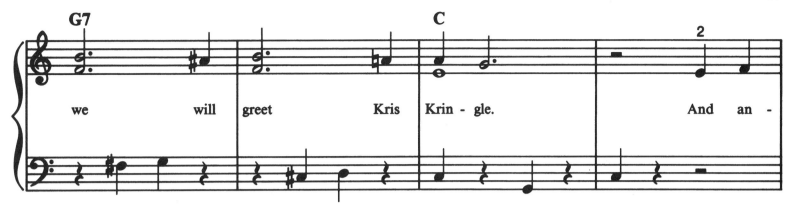

we will greet Kris Krin - gle. And an -

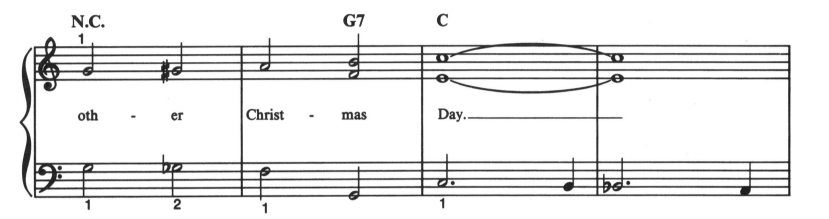

oth - er Christ - mas Day.

Come one and dance the
dance the

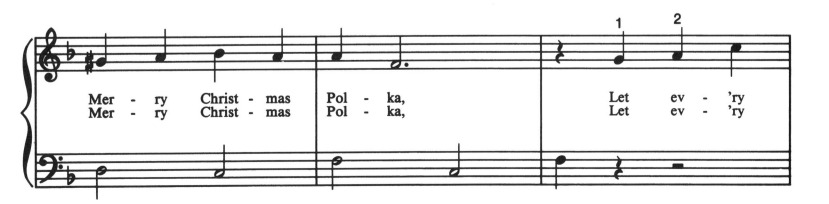

Mer - ry Christ - mas Pol - ka, Let ev - 'ry
Mer - ry Christ - mas Pol - ka, Let ev - 'ry

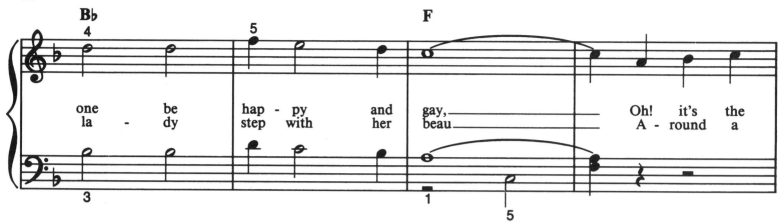

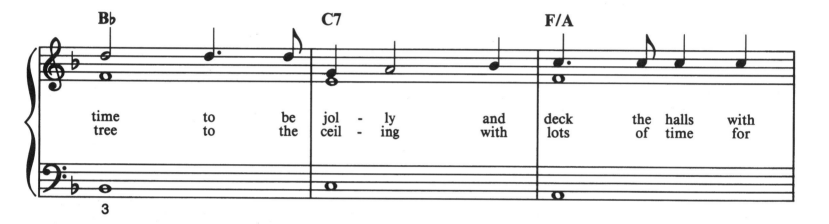

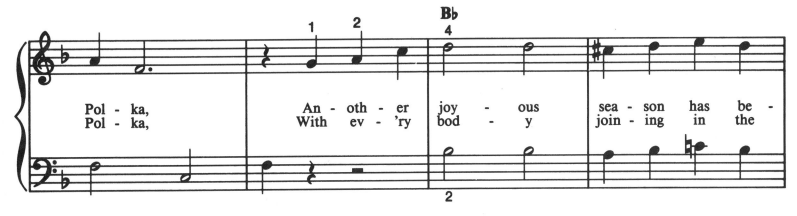

Pol - ka,
Pol - ka,

An - oth - er joy - ous sea - son has be -
With ev - 'ry bod - y join - ing in the

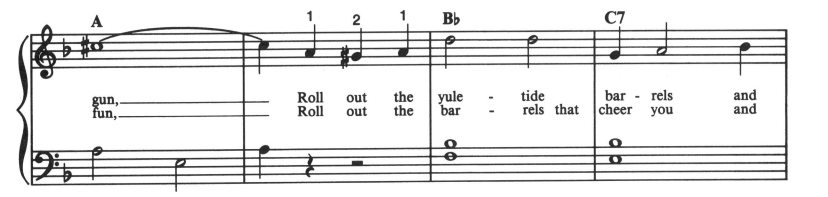

gun, _____
fun, _____

Roll out the yule - tide bar - rels and
Roll out the bar - rels that cheer you and

sing out the car - ols, A mer - ry Christ - mas ev - 'r'y
shout 'til they hear you,

one!
Come on and

one!

MERRY CHRISTMAS, DARLING

Words and Music by RICHARD CARPENTER
and FRANK POOLER

Freely, rubato

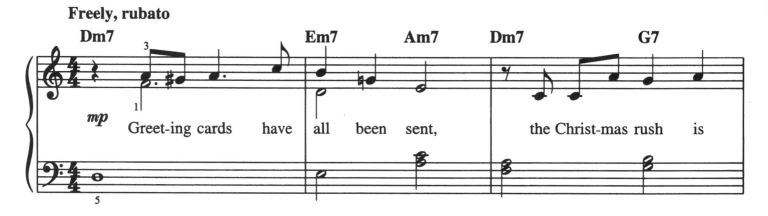

Greet-ing cards have all been sent, the Christ-mas rush is

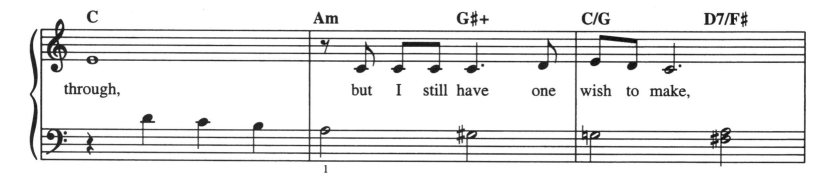

through, but I still have one wish to make,

Moderately slow

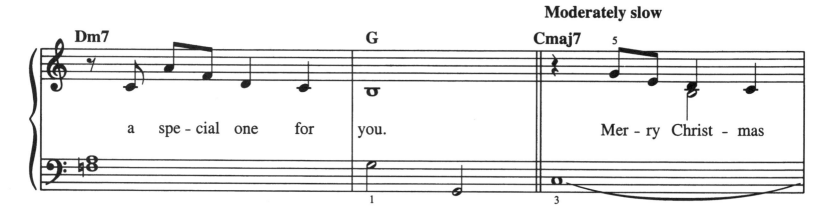

a spe-cial one for you. Mer-ry Christ-mas

Dm/C — Cmaj7 — Am7 — Gm7 — C7

dar - ling. We're a - part that's true; but

F — G/F — Em7 — Am7 — Dm7 — Em

I can dream and in my dreams, I'm Christ - mas - ing with

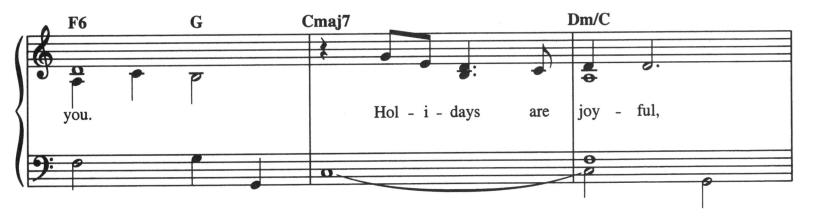

F6 — G — Cmaj7 — Dm/C

you. Hol - i - days are joy - ful,

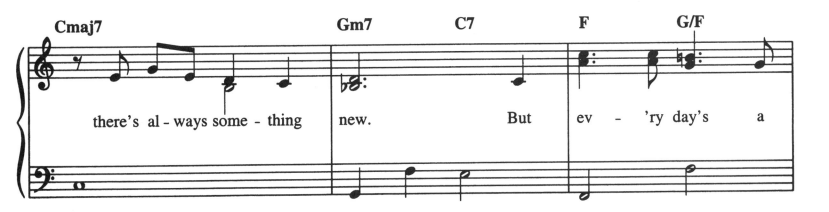

Cmaj7 — Gm7 — C7 — F — G/F

there's al - ways some - thing new. But ev - 'ry day's a

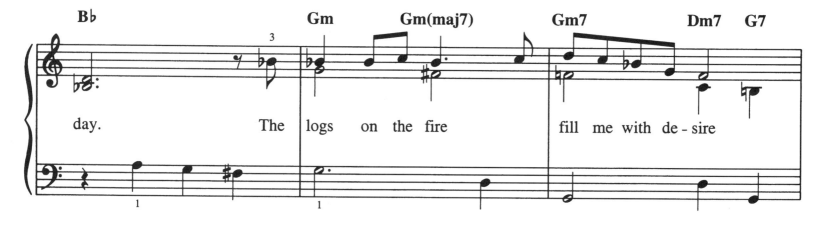

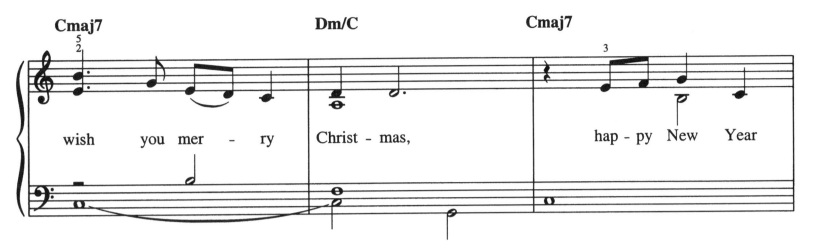

THE MOST WONDERFUL DAY OF THE YEAR

Music and Lyrics by
JOHNNY MARKS

Moderately

With Pedal

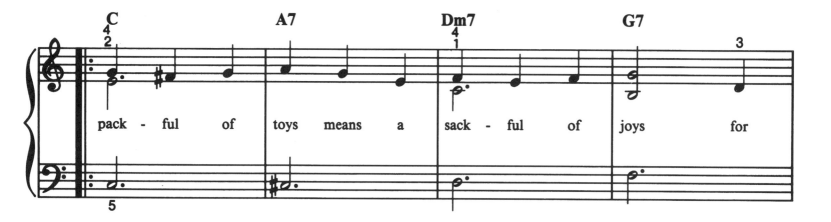

pack - ful of toys means a sack - ful of joys for

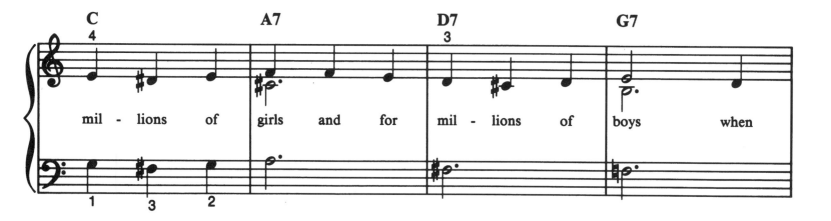

mil - lions of girls and for mil - lions of boys when

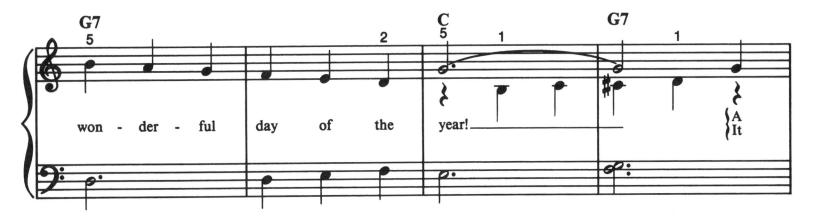

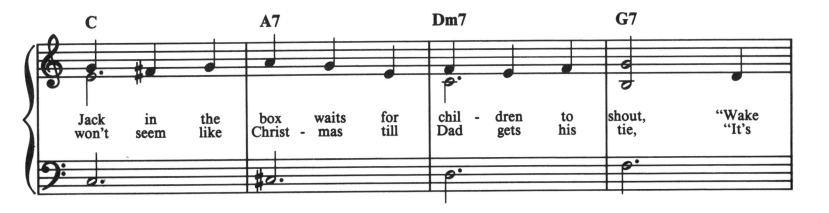

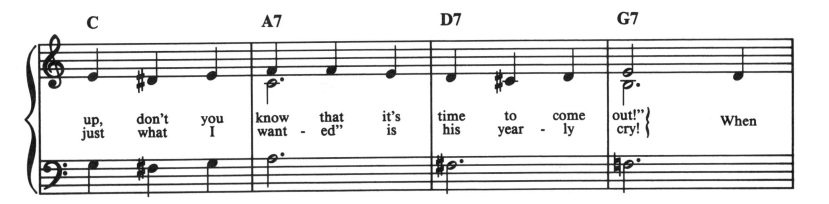

C   **Cdim**   **C**   **C#dim7**

Christ - mas Day   is   here _____   The most

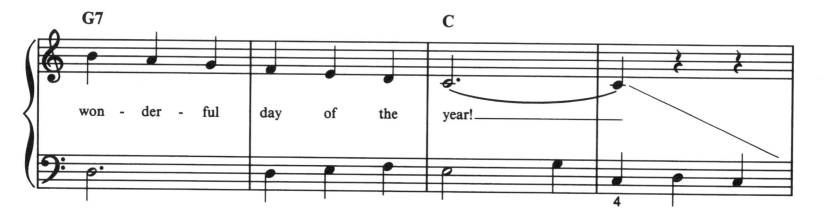

G7   **C**

won - der - ful   day   of the   year! _____

G7   3
          1

{ Toys   ga -   lore _____   scat - tered
  Spir   its   gay _____   ev' - ry -

Melody

C   3
          1

on   the   floor. _____   There's   no
one   will   say _____   Hap -   py

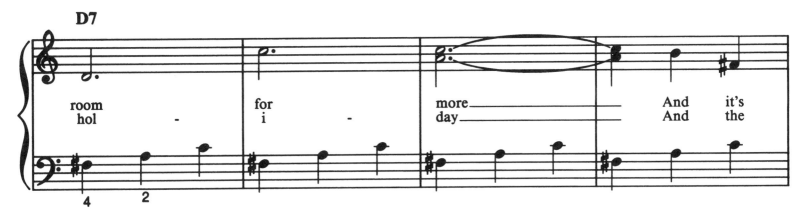

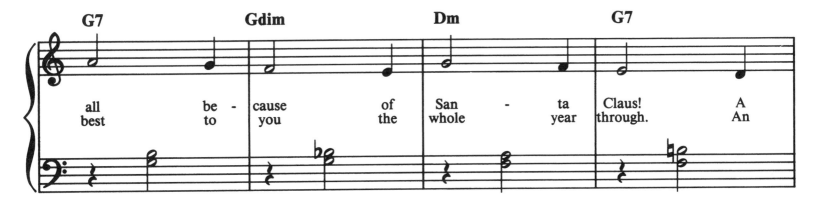

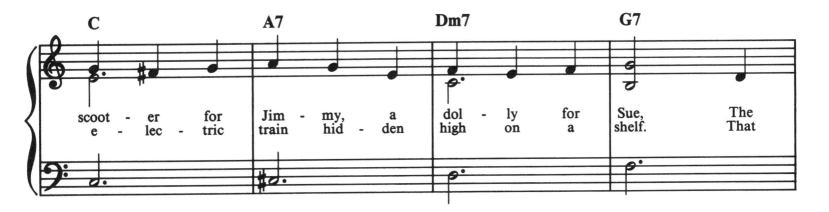

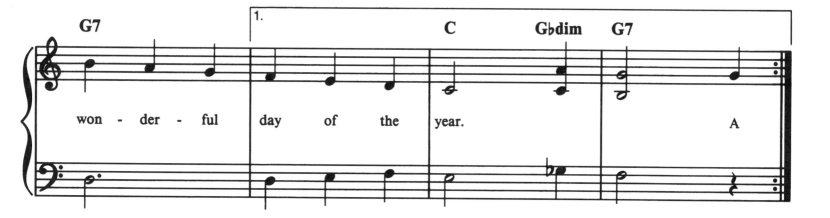

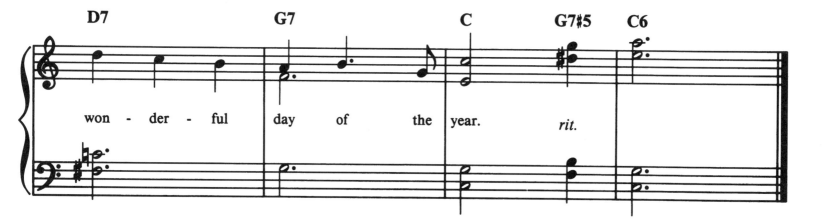

O CHRISTMAS TREE

Traditional German Carol

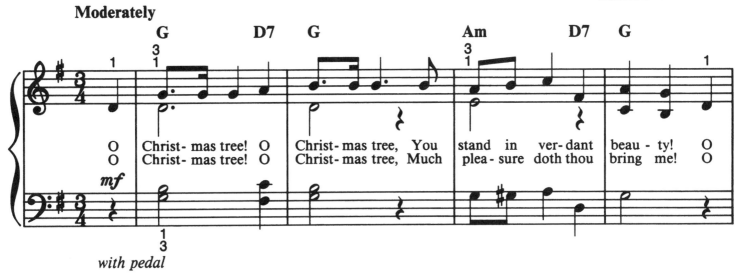

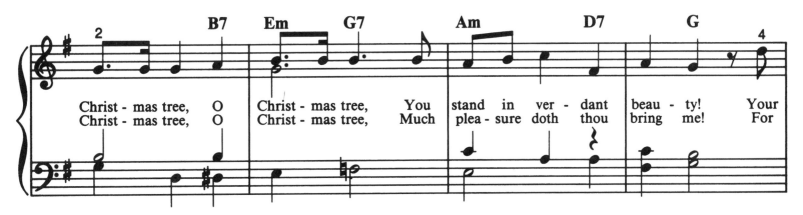

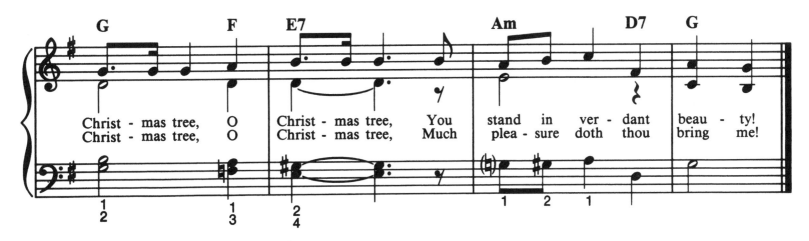

NUTTIN' FOR CHRISTMAS

Words and Music by ROY BENNETT
and SID TEPPER

Moderately fast

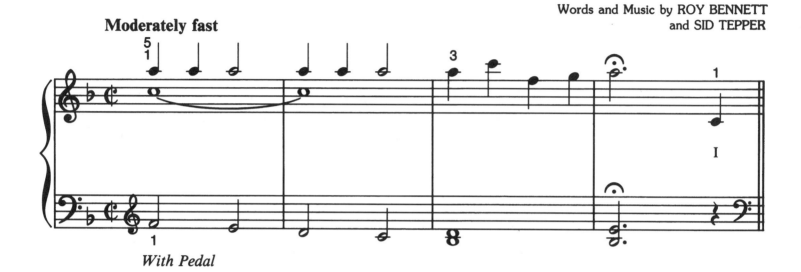

With Pedal

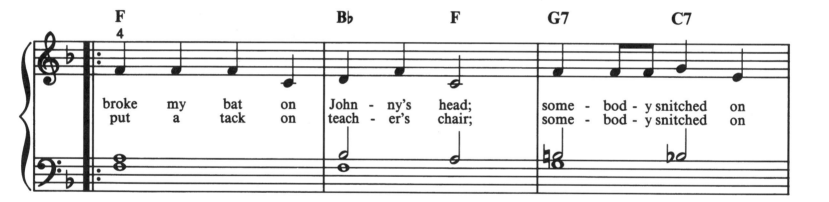

| F | | | Bb | F | G7 | C7 |

broke my bat on John - ny's head; some - bod - y snitched on
put a tack on teach - er's chair; some - bod - y snitched on

| F | | | | Bb | F |

me. I hid a frog in sis - ter's bed;
me. I tied a knot in Su - sie's hair;

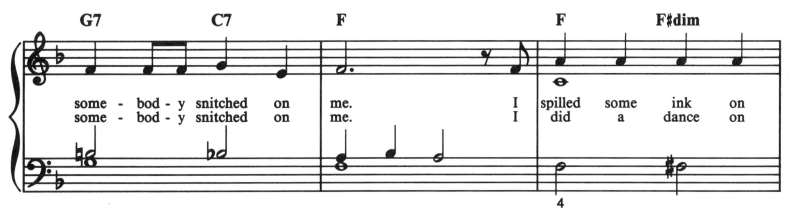

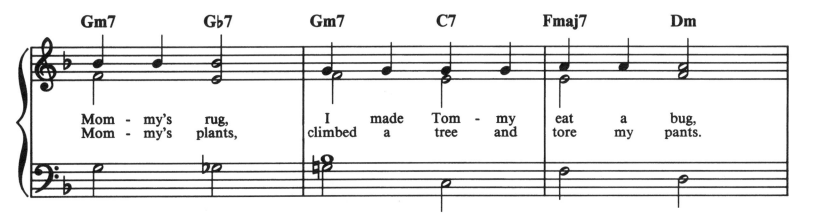

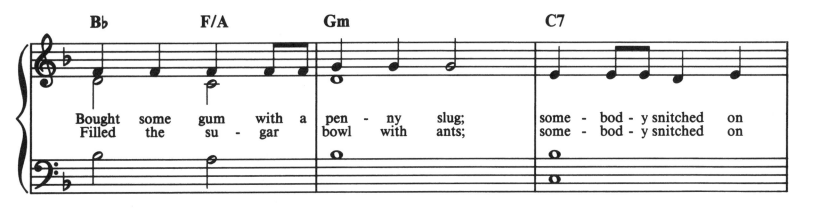

112

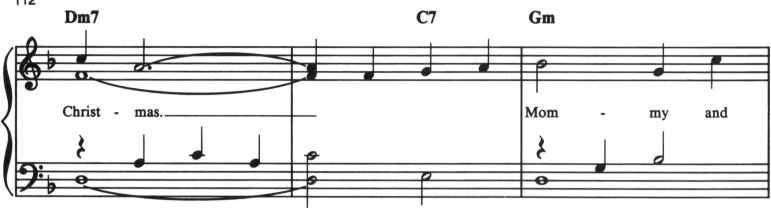

Christ - mas.____ Mom - my and

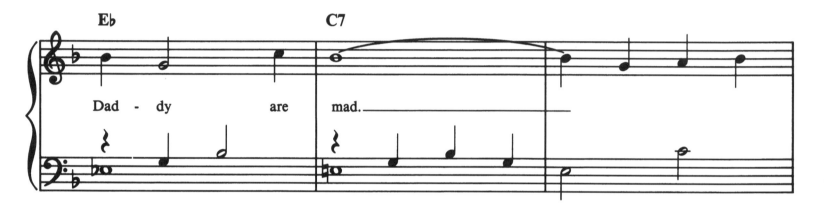

Dad - dy are mad.____ I'm get - tin' nut - tin' for Christ - mas,____

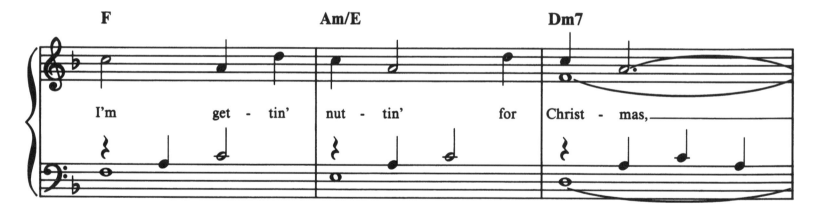

____ 'Cause I ain't been nut - tin' but

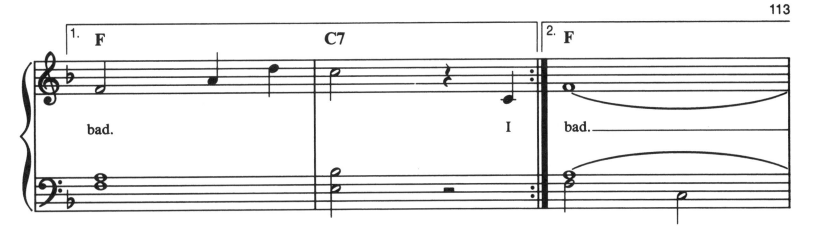

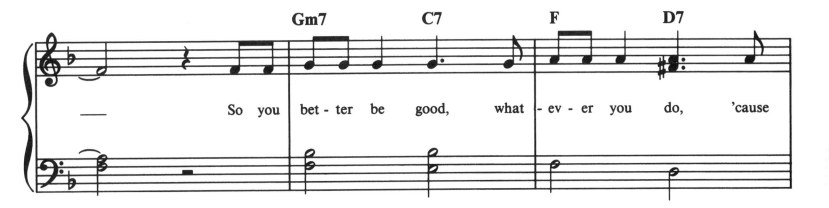

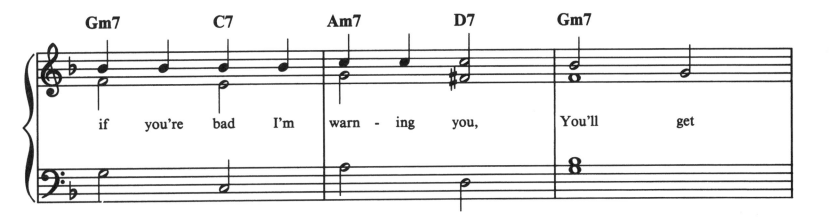

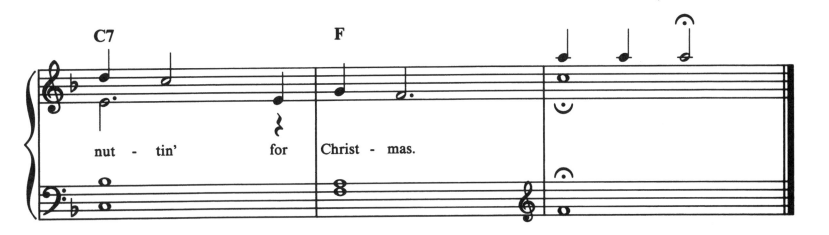

O COME, ALL YE FAITHFUL
(Adeste Fideles)

Words and Music by JOHN FRANCIS WADE
Latin Words translated by FREDERICK OAKELEY

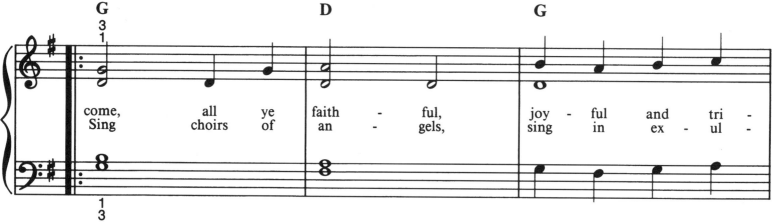

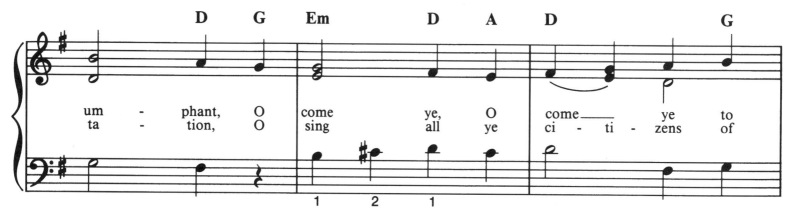

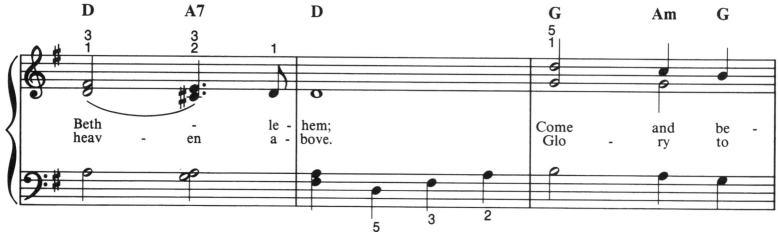

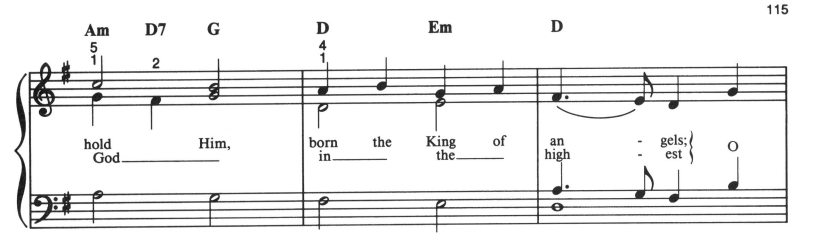

O COME, O COME IMMANUEL

Plainsong, 13th Century
Words translated by JOHN M. NEALE
and HENRY S. COFFIN

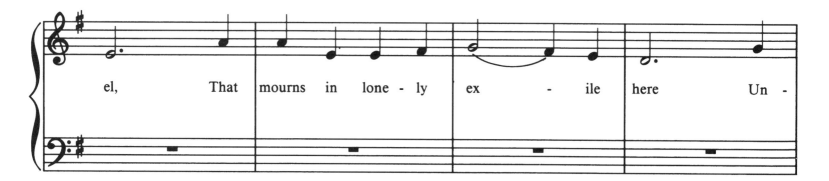

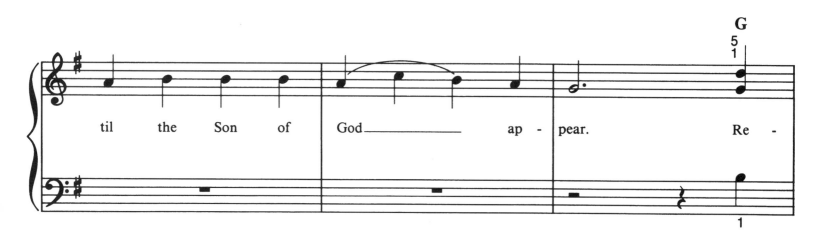

117

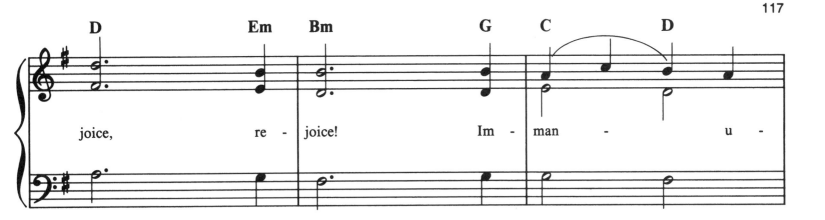

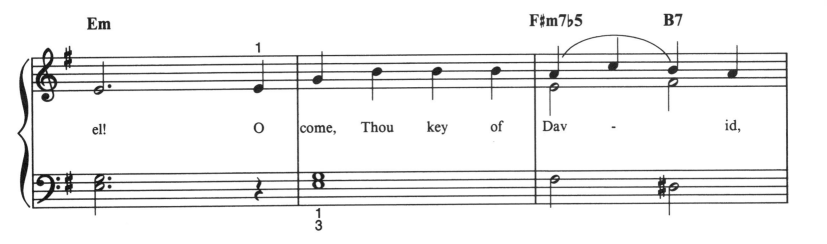

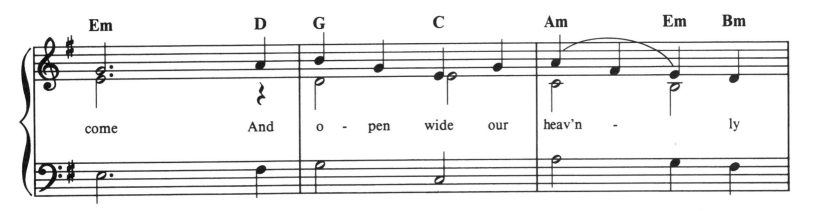

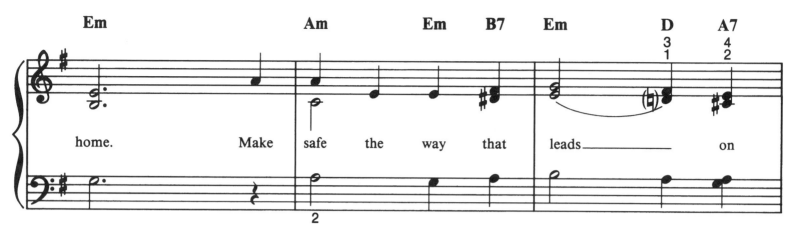

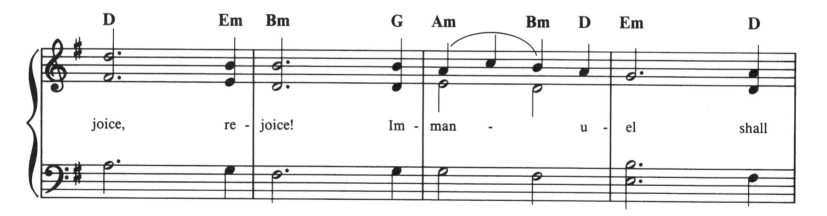

PRETTY PAPER

Words and Music by
WILLIE NELSON

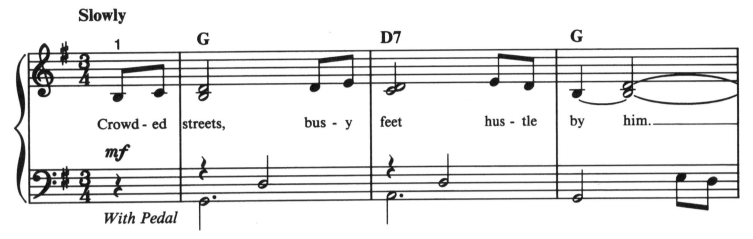

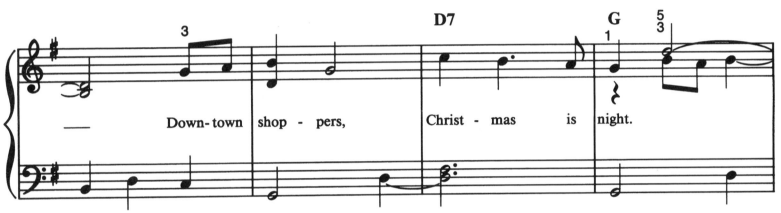

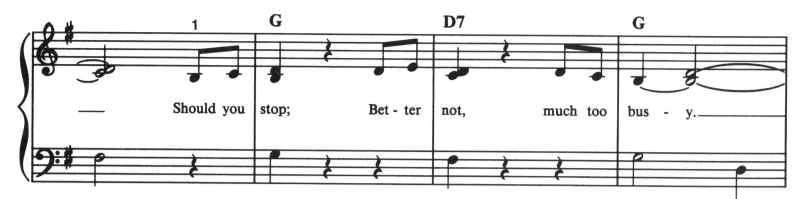

Should you stop; Bet - ter not, much too bus - y.

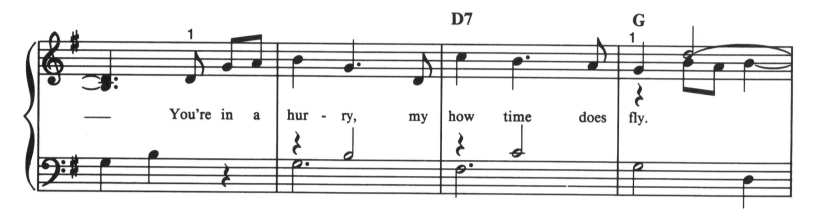

You're in a hur - ry, my how time does fly.

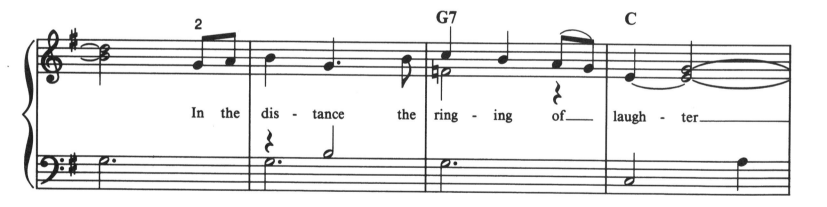

In the dis - tance the ring - ing of laugh - ter

And in the midst of the laugh - ter he cries.

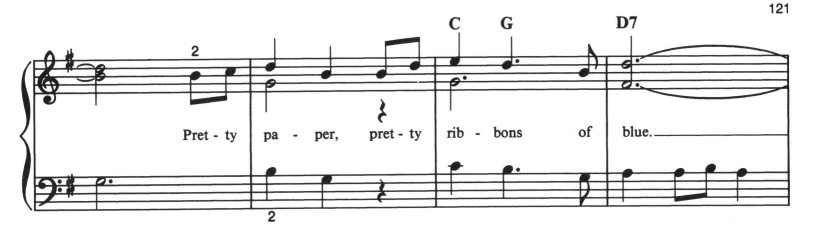

Pret - ty pa - per, pret - ty rib - bons of blue.___

___ Wrap your pres - ents to your dar - ling from you.___

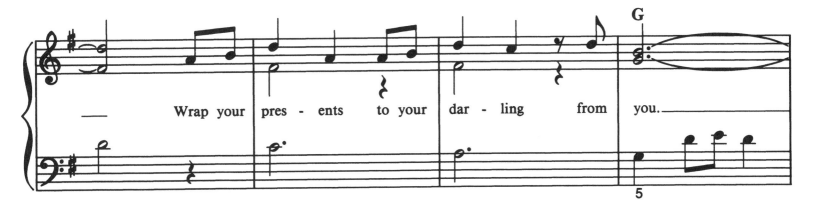

___ Pret - ty pen - cils to write, "I love you."___

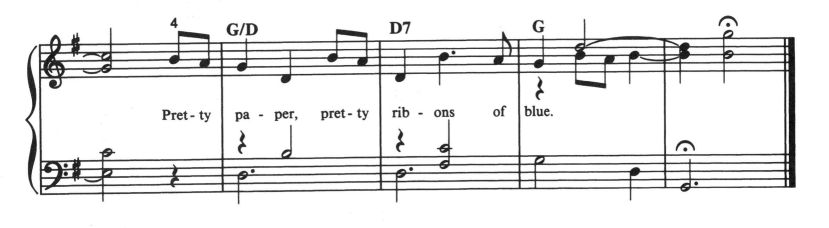

Pret - ty pa - per, pret - ty rib - ons of blue.

O HOLY NIGHT

French Words by PLACIDE CAPPEAU
English Words by JOHN S. DWIGHT
Music by ADOLPHE ADAM

Slow and flowing

mp

with pedal

O ho - ly night_____ the

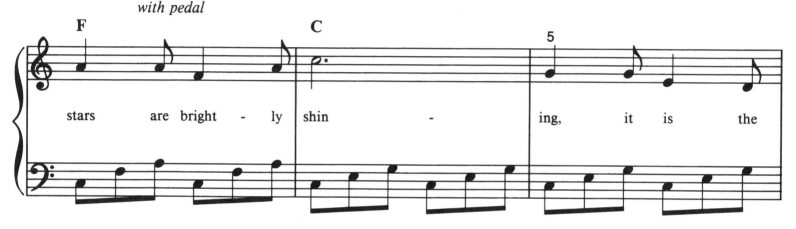

stars are bright - ly shin - ing, it is the

night of the dear Sav - ior's birth;_____

_____ Long lay the world_____ in

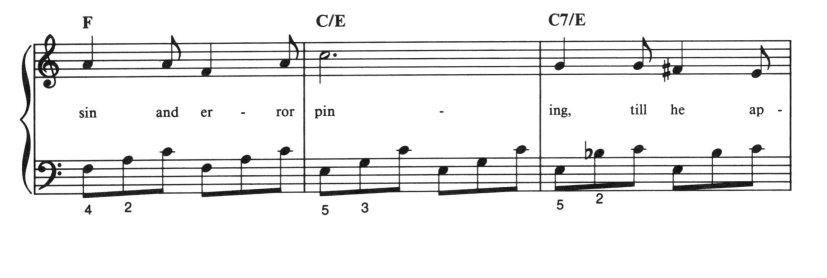

sin and er - ror pin - ing, till he ap -

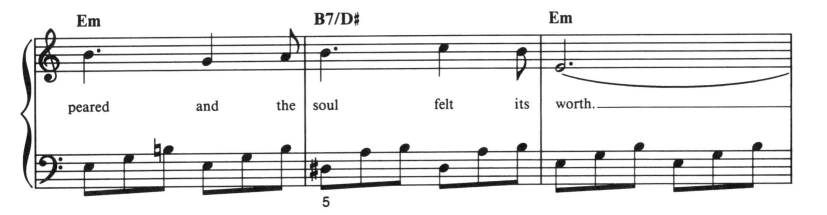

peared and the soul felt its worth.

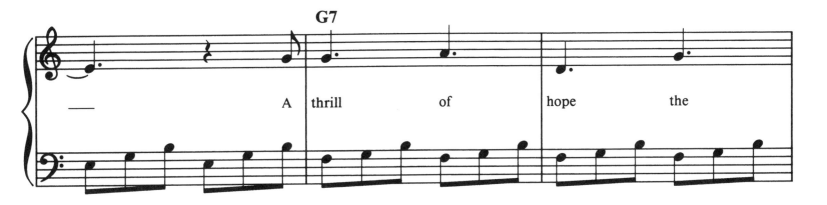

A thrill of hope the

wea - ry soul re - joic - es, for yon - der

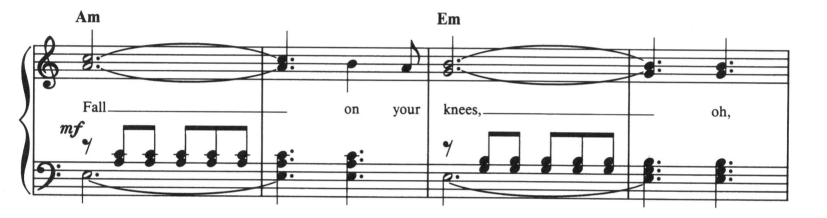

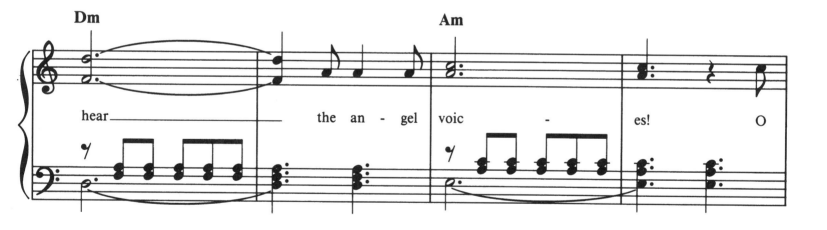

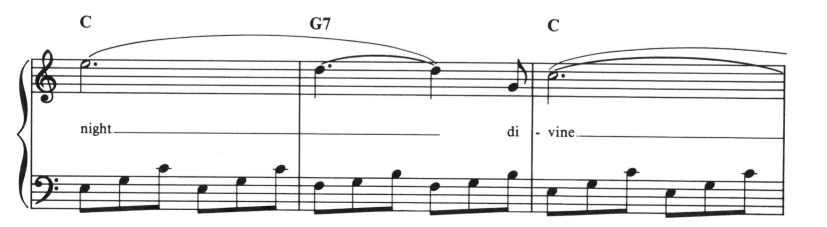

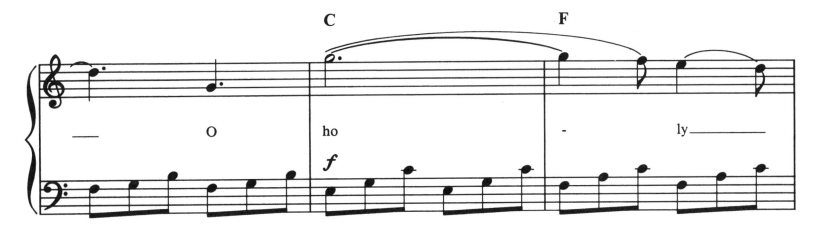

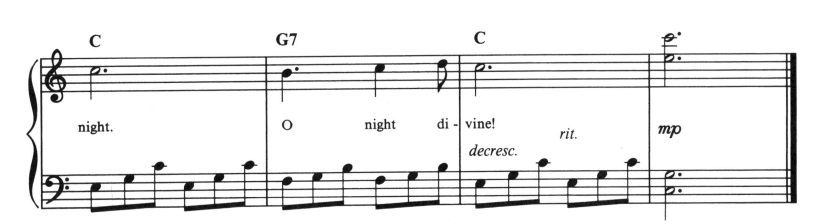

O LITTLE TOWN OF BETHLEHEM

Words by PHILLIPS BROOKS
Music by LEWIS H. REDNER

Slowly

mp

with pedal

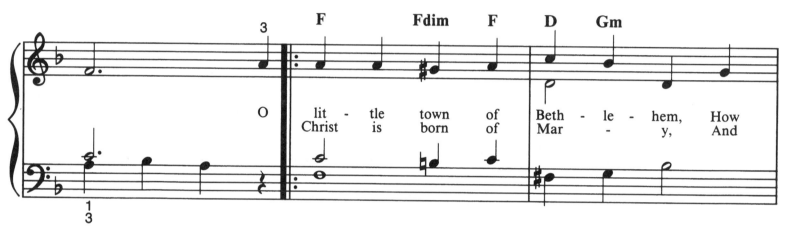

O
Christ is town born of

lit - tle town of
Mar - y, How And

Beth - le - hem, How

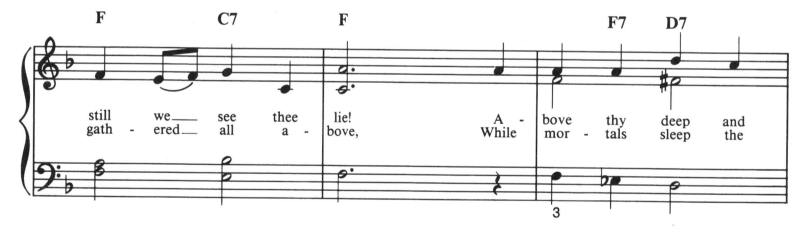

still we___ see thee lie! A - bove thy deep and
gath - ered___ all a - bove, While mor - tals sleep and the

dream - less sleep The si - lent___ stars go
an - gels keep Their watch of___ won - d'ring

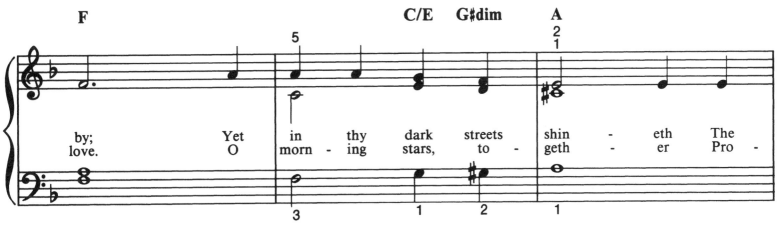

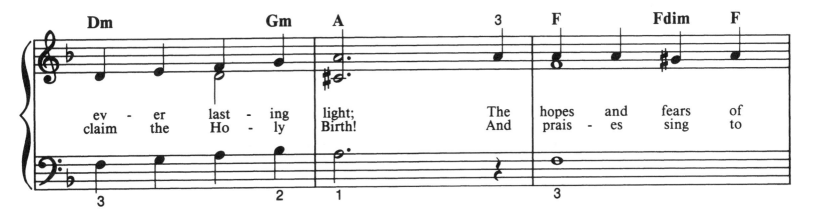

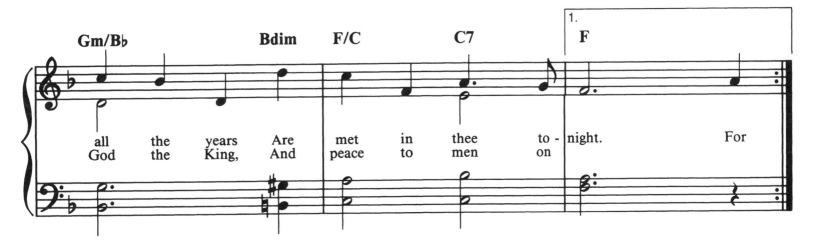

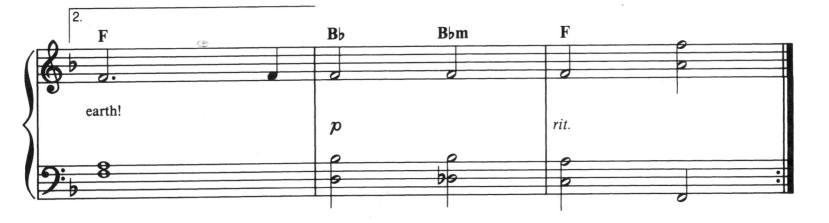

O SANCTISSIMA

Sicilian Carol

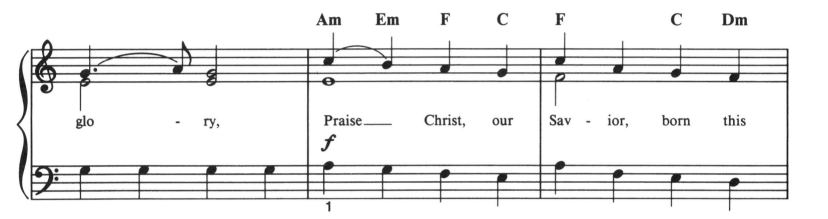

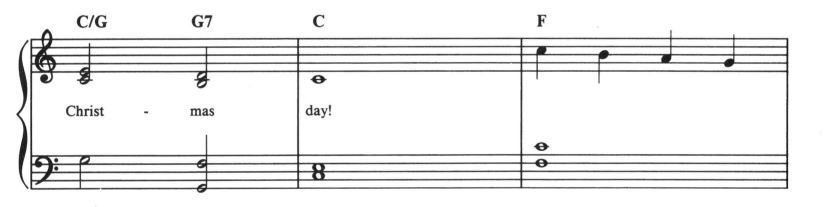

PARADE OF THE WOODEN SOLDIERS

English Lyrics by BALLARD MacDONALD
Music by LEON JESSEL

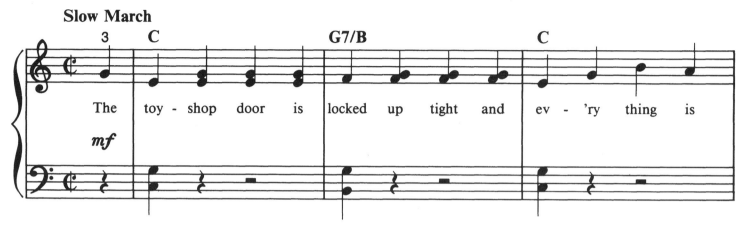

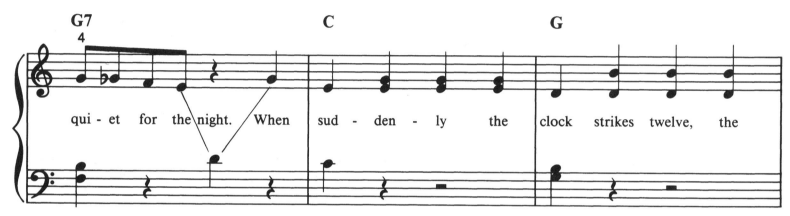

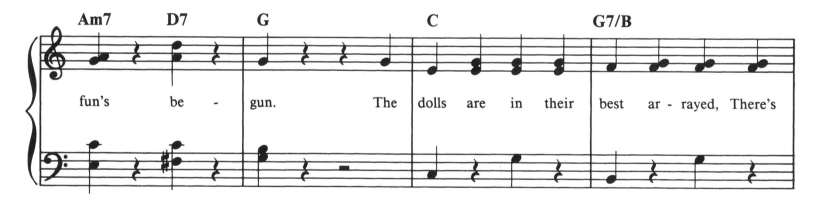

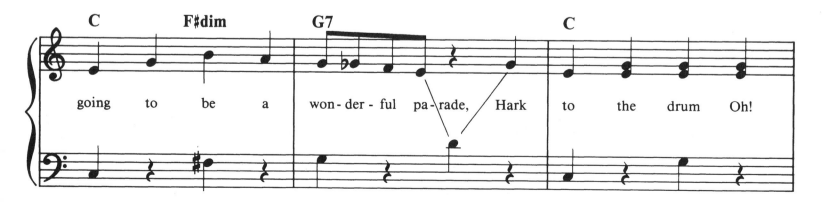

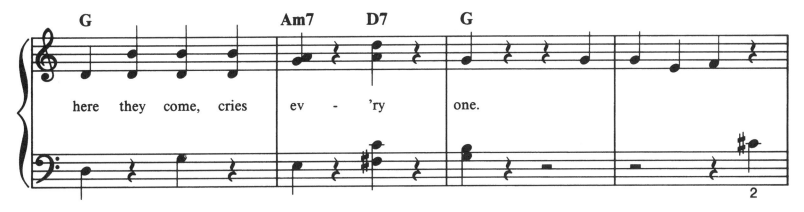

here they come, cries ev - 'ry one.

Hear them all cheer - ing, Now they are near - ing,

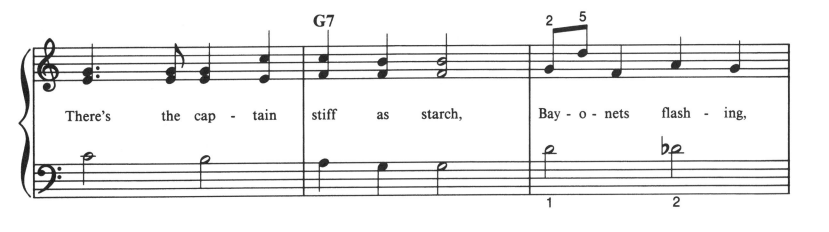

There's the cap - tain stiff as starch, Bay - o - nets flash - ing,

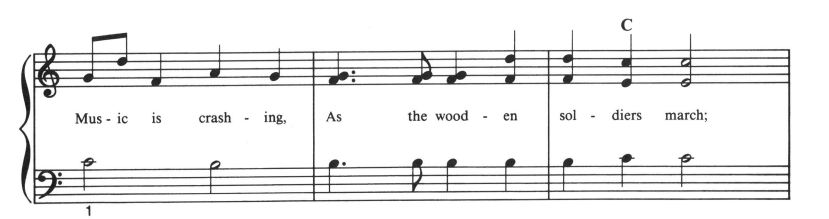

Mus - ic is crash - ing, As the wood - en sol - diers march;

132

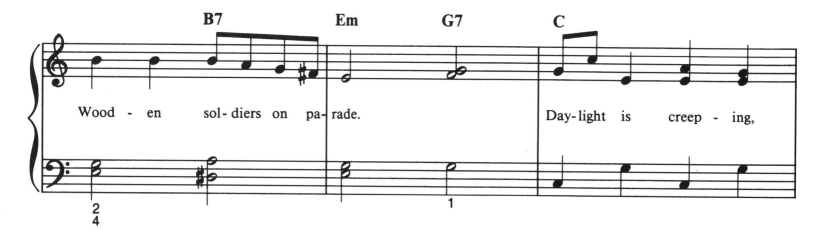

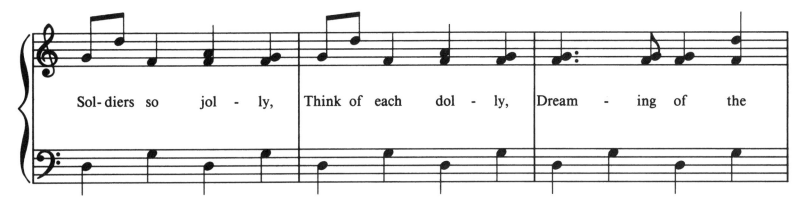

Sol- diers so jol - ly, Think of each dol - ly, Dream - ing of the

C

night that's past; When in the morn - ing, with-out a warn - ing,

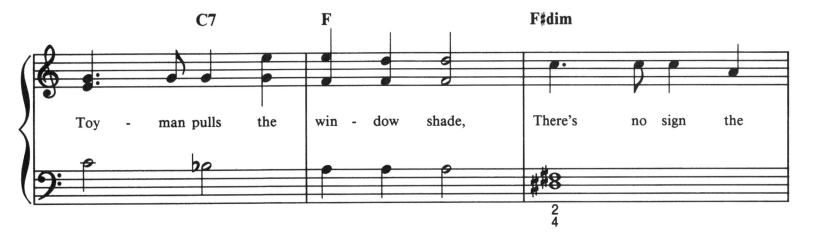

C7   **F**   **F♯dim**

Toy - man pulls the win - dow shade, There's no sign the

$\frac{2}{4}$

C/E   **A7/C♯**   **Dm**   **G7**   **C**

Wood bri - gade was ev - er out up - on pa - rade.

ROCKIN' AROUND THE CHRISTMAS TREE

Music and Lyrics by
JOHNNY MARKS

Moderate rock

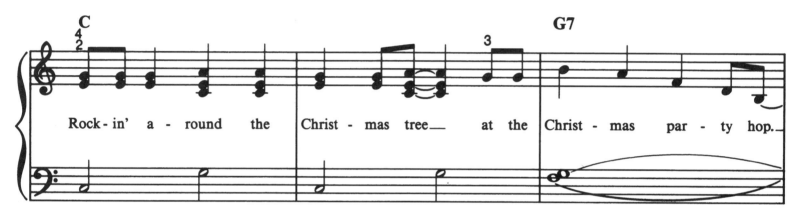

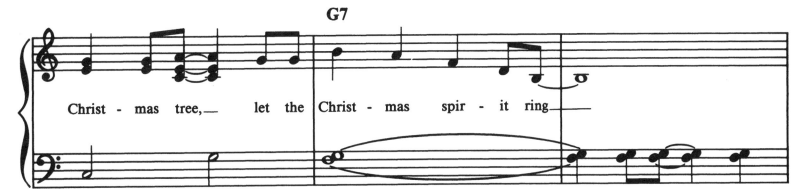

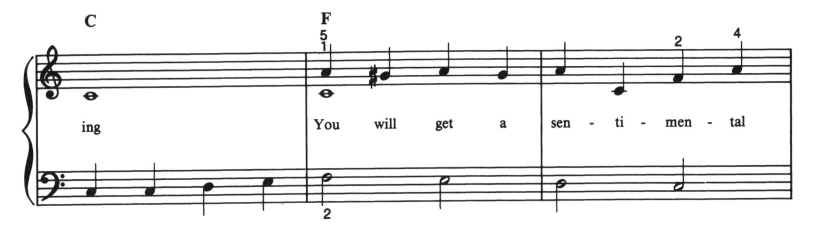

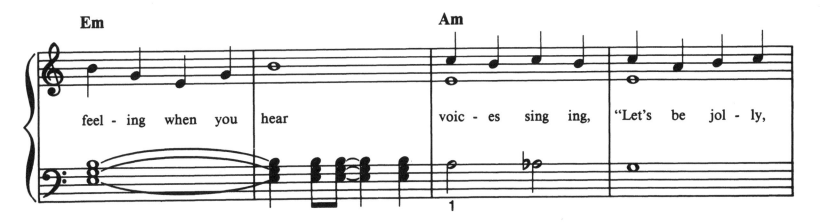

136

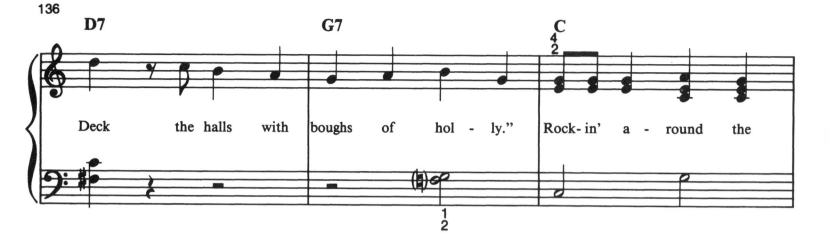

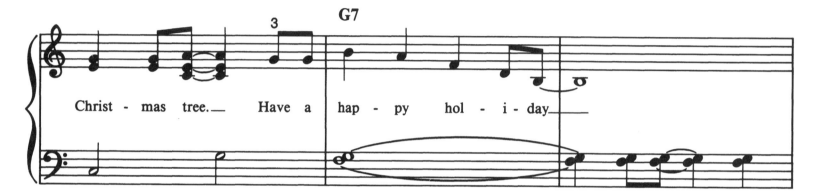

RUDOLPH THE RED-NOSED REINDEER

Music and Lyrics by
JOHNNY MARKS

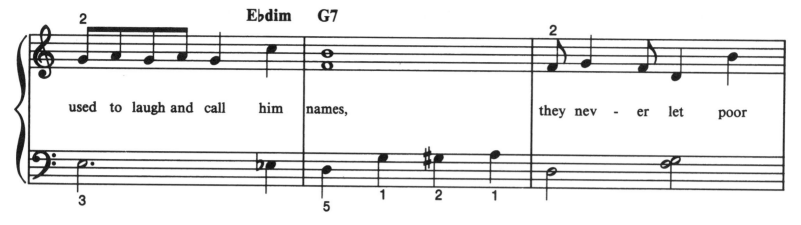

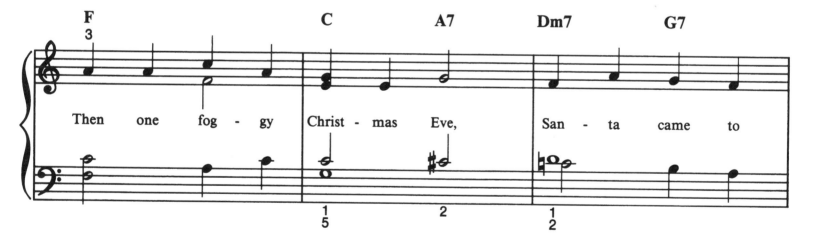

won't you guide my sleigh to-night?" Then how the rein - deer

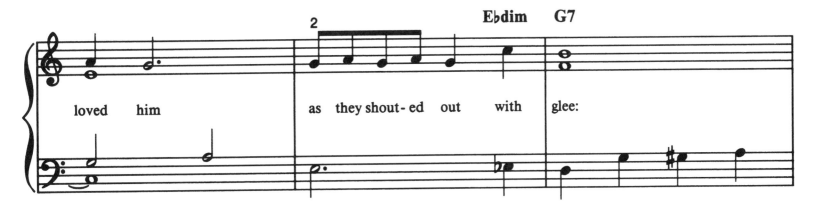

loved him as they shout-ed out with glee:

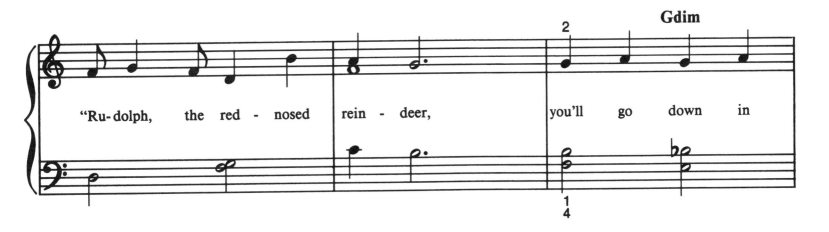

"Ru-dolph, the red - nosed rein - deer, you'll go down in

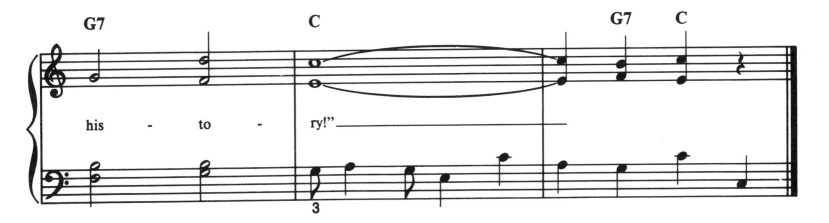

his - to - ry!"

SILENT NIGHT

Words by JOSEPH MOHR
Translated by JOHN F. YOUNG
Music by FRANZ X. GRUBER

Slowly

with pedal

Si - lent night,   ho - ly night!
Si - lent night,   ho - ly night!

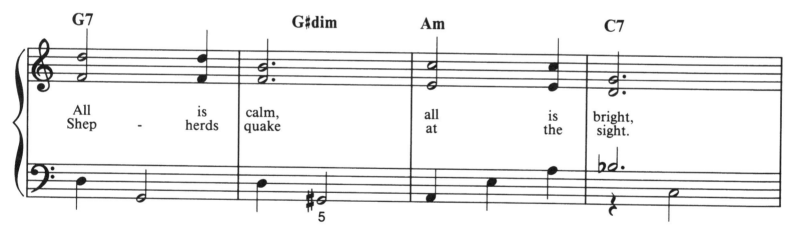

All   is   calm,   all   is   bright,
Shep - herds   quake   at   the   sight.

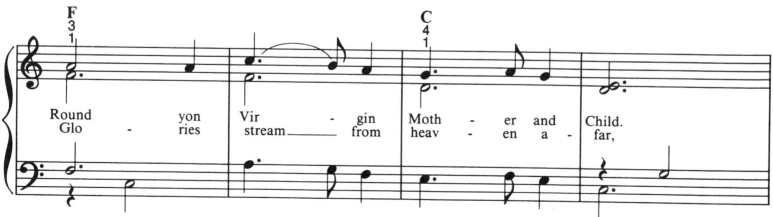

Round   yon   Vir - gin   Moth - er   and   Child.
Glo - ries   stream____ from   heav - en   a - far,

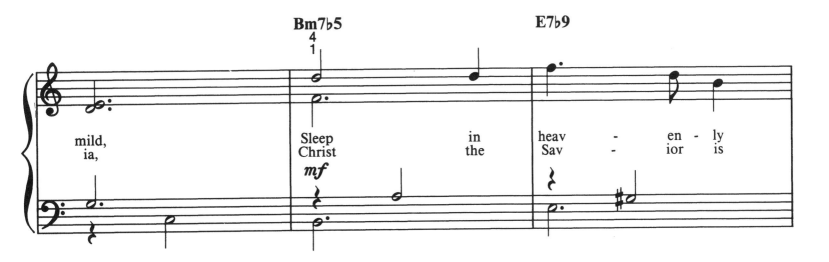

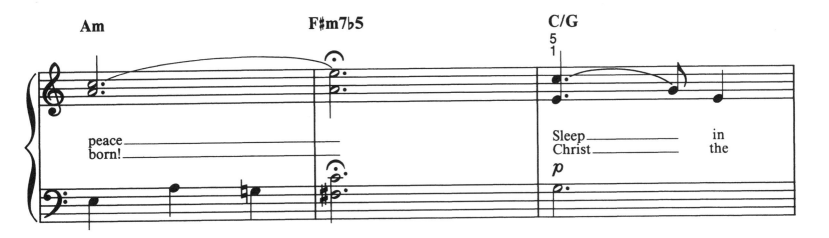

141

SILVER AND GOLD

Music and Lryics by
JOHNNY MARKS

Slowly

With Pedal

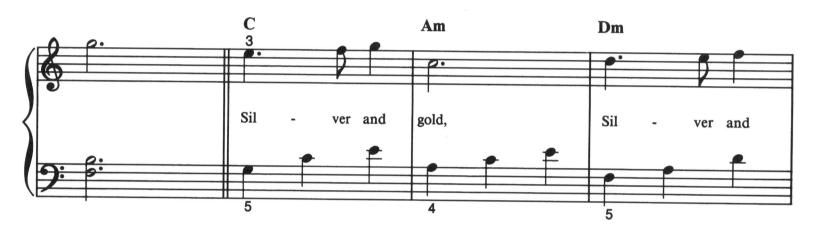

Sil - ver and gold, Sil - ver and

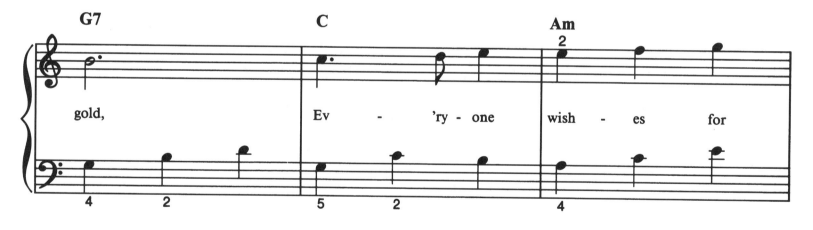

gold, Ev - 'ry-one wish - es for

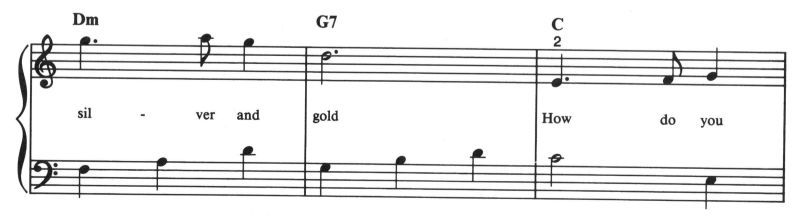

sil - ver and gold How do you

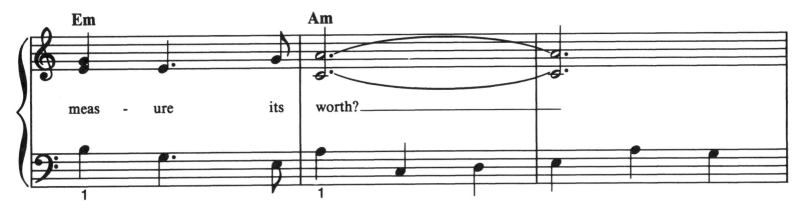

meas - ure   its   worth?

Just   by the   pleas - ure   it   gives   here   on

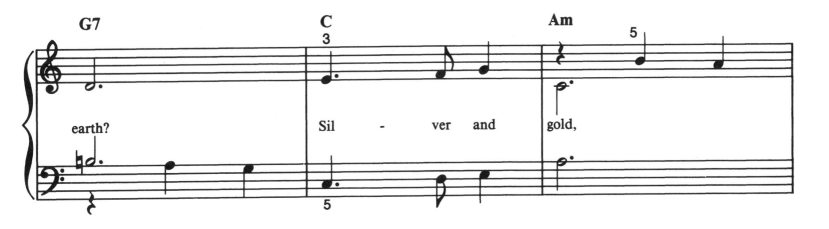

earth?   Sil - ver and   gold,

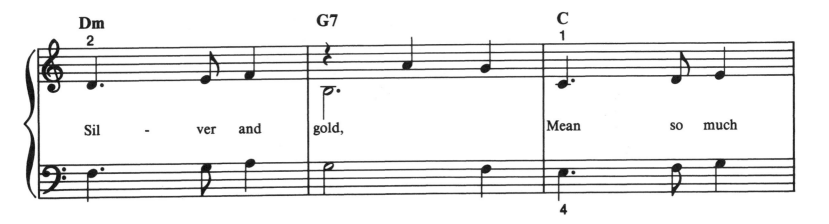

Sil - ver and   gold,   Mean   so   much

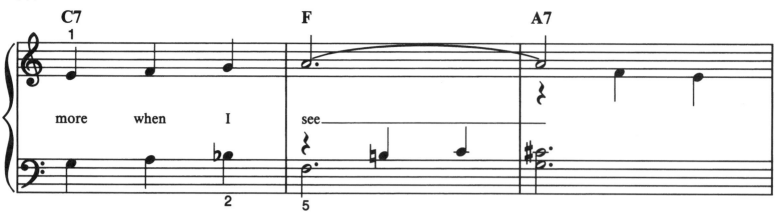

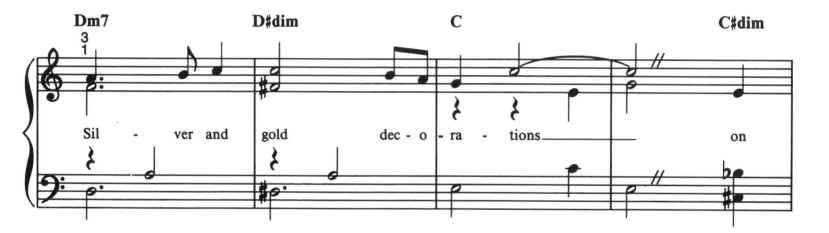

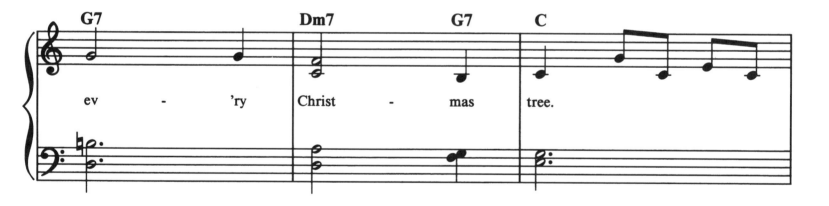

SILVER BELLS
from the Paramount Picture THE LEMON DROP KID

Words and Music by JAY LIVINGSTON
and RAY EVANS

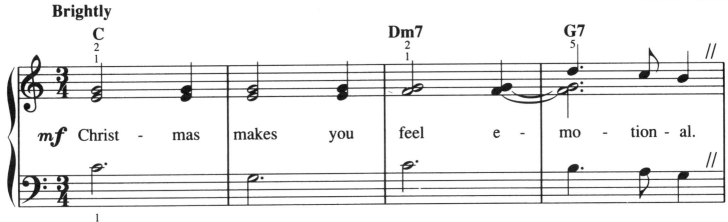

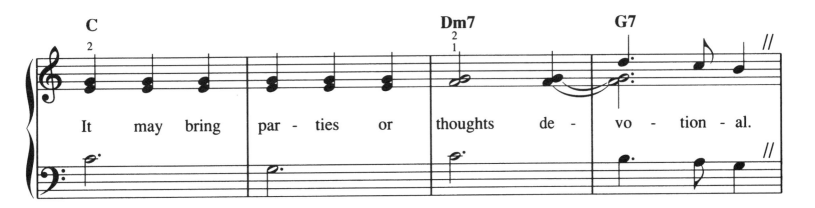

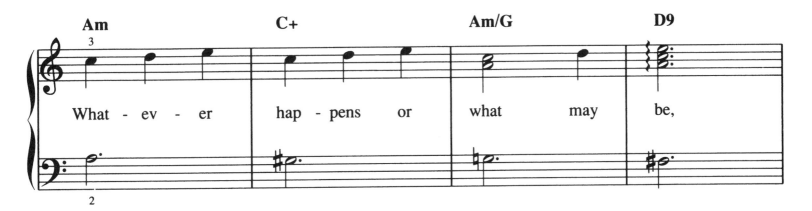

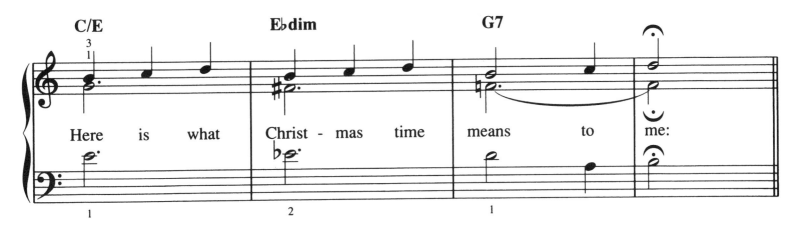

146

Chorus
Moderately

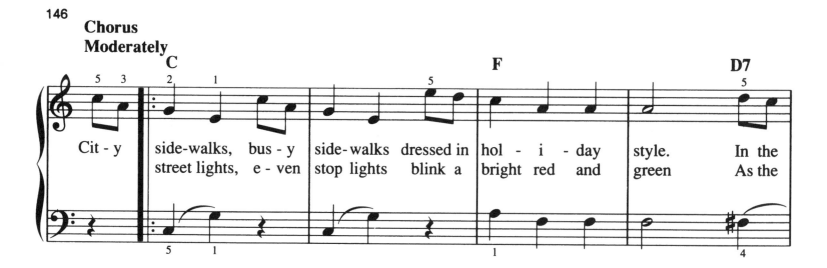

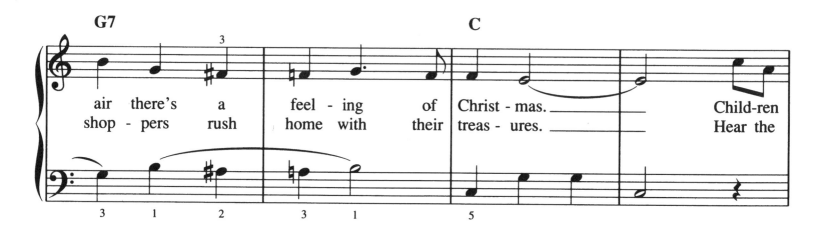

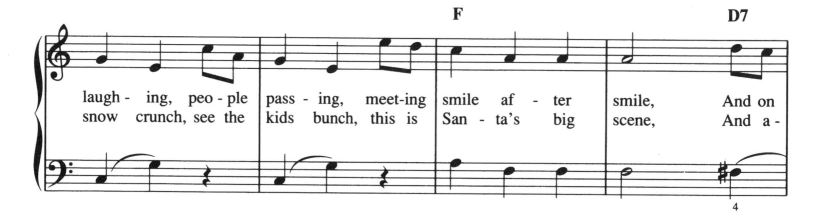

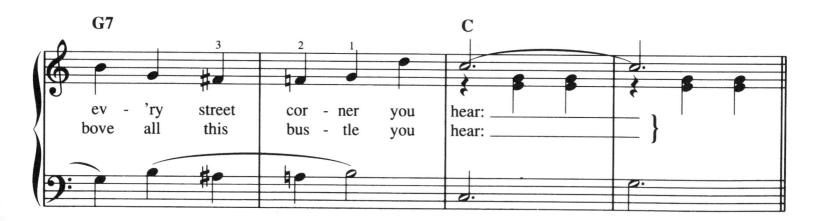

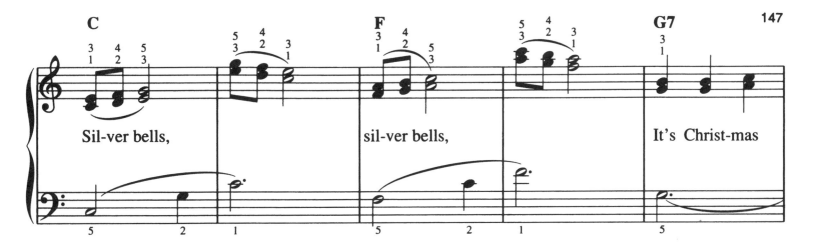

Sil-ver bells,   sil-ver bells,   It's Christ-mas

time   in the cit - y.   Ring-a-ling,

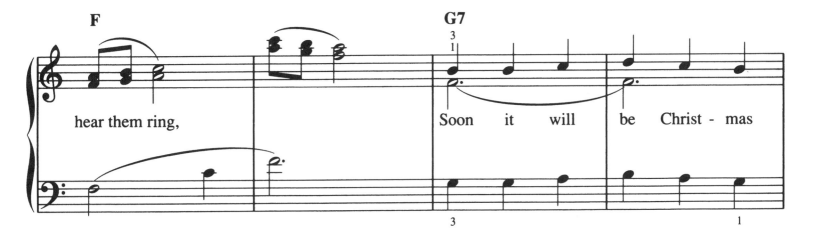

hear them ring,   Soon   it will   be   Christ - mas

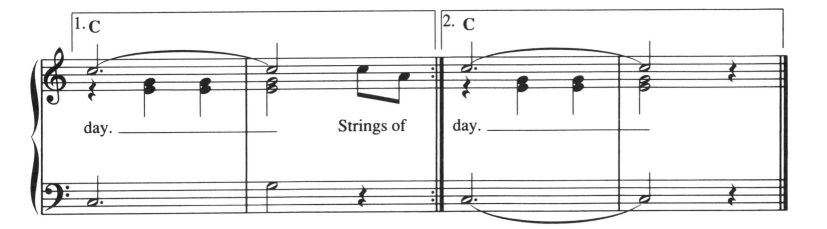

day.   Strings of   day.

SUZY SNOWFLAKE

Words and Music by SID TEPPER
and ROY BENNETT

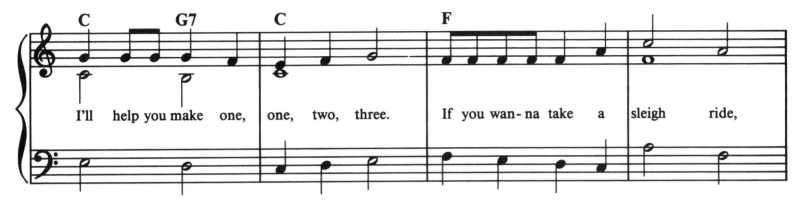

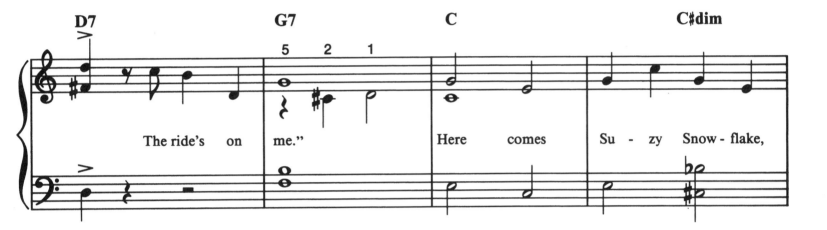

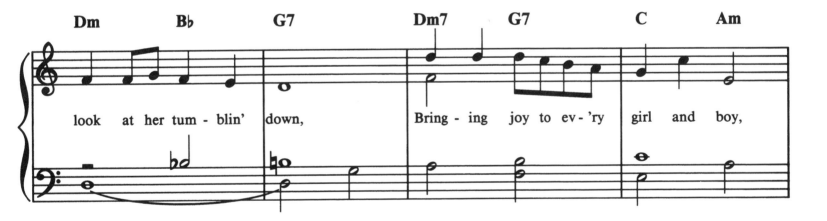

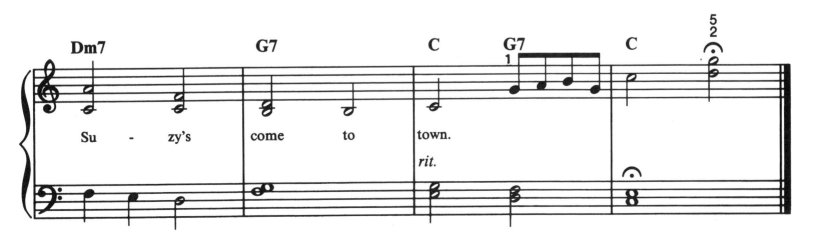

TOYLAND
from BABES IN TOYLAND

Words by GLEN MACDONOUGH
Music by VICTOR HERBERT

Moderately

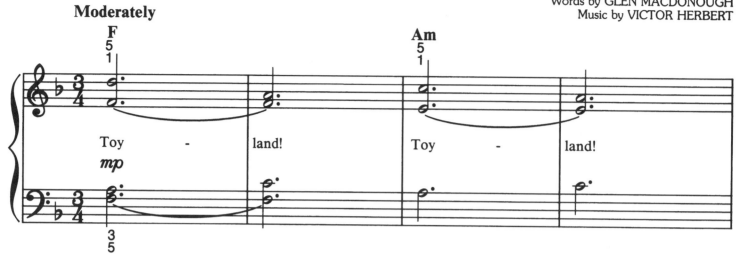

Toy - land! Toy - land!

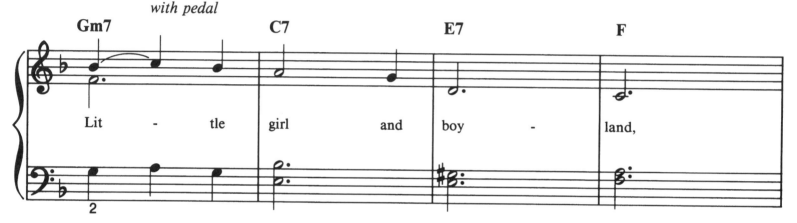

Lit - tle girl and boy - land,

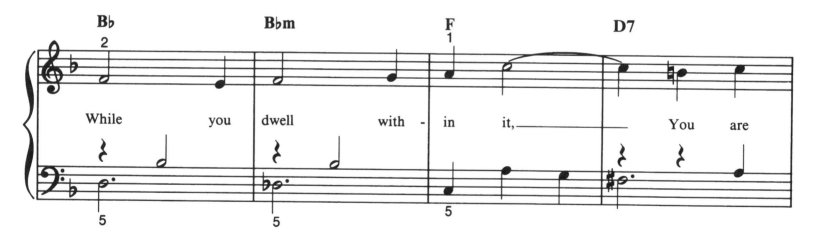

While you dwell with - in it, You are

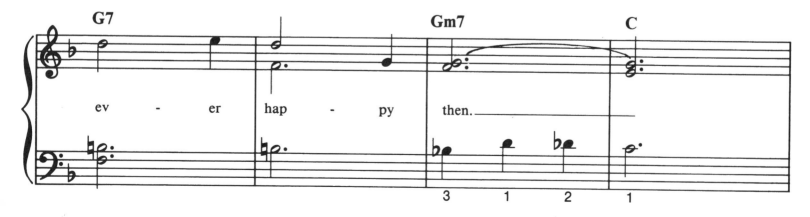

ev - er hap - py then.

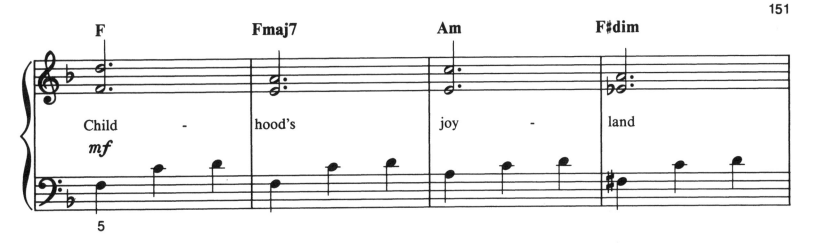

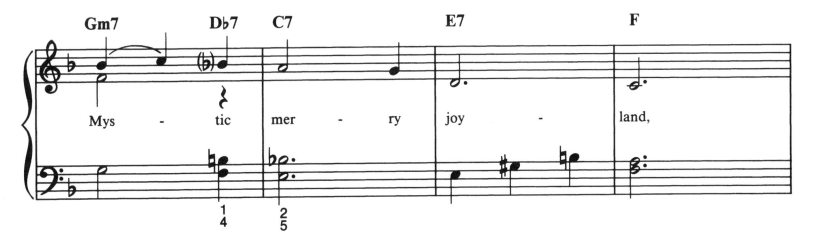

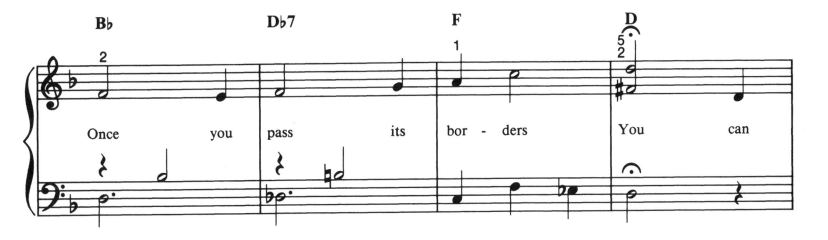

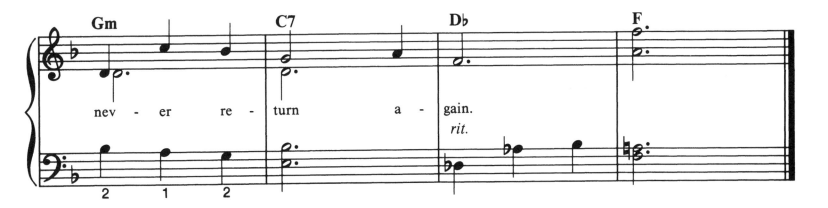

UP ON THE HOUSETOP

Words and Music by
B.R. HANDY

Brightly

Up on the house-top

rein-deer pause, Out jumps good old San-ta Claus; Down thru the chim-ney with

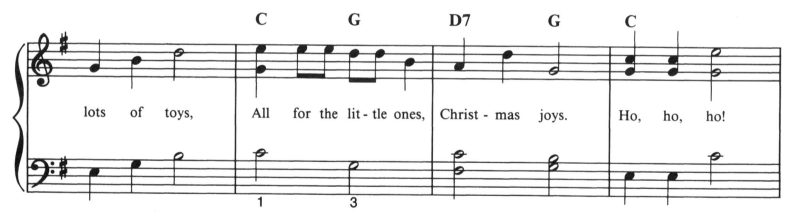

lots of toys, All for the lit-tle ones, Christ-mas joys. Ho, ho, ho!

Who would-n't go! Ho, ho, ho! Who would-n't go!

153

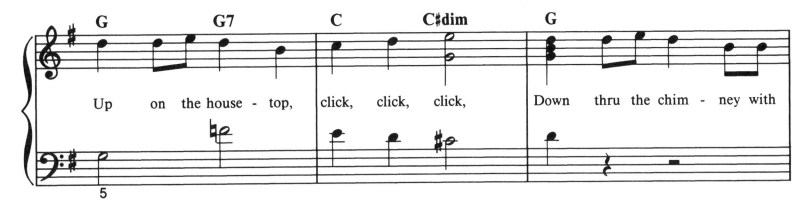

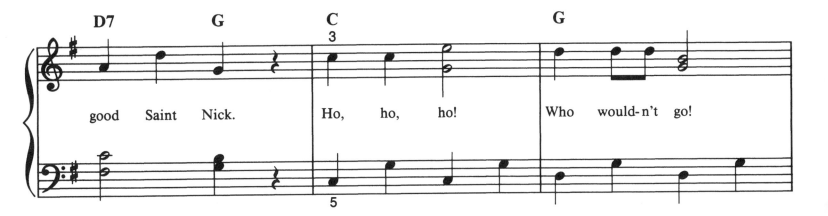

WE THREE KINGS OF ORIENT ARE

Words and Music by
JOHN H. HOPKINS, JR.

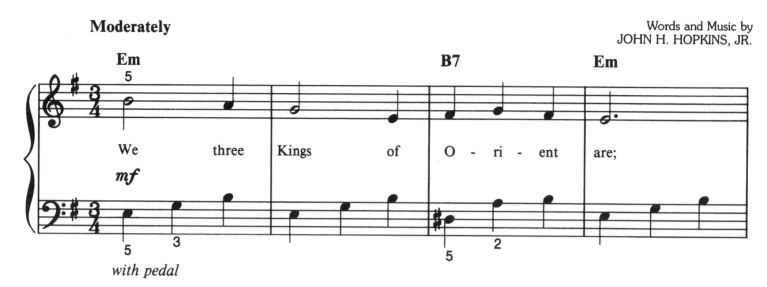

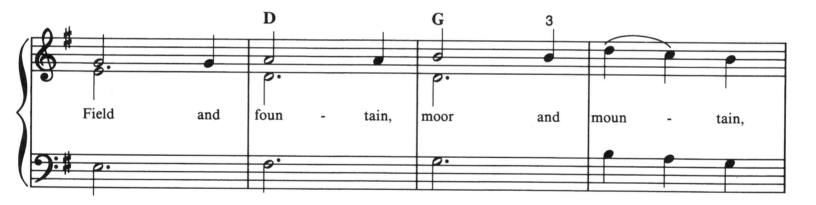

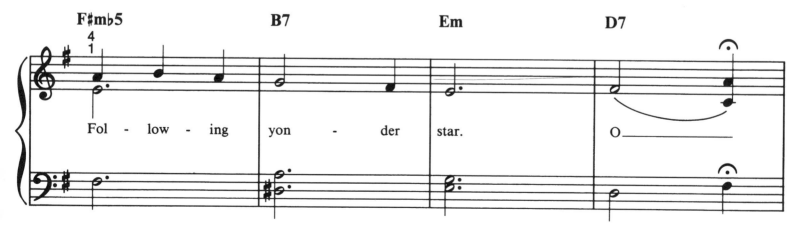

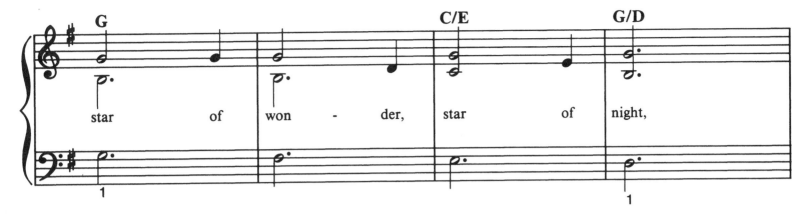

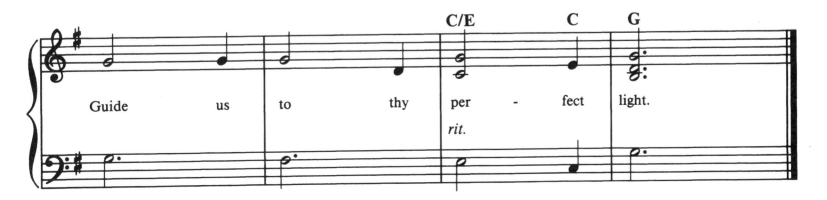

WE WISH YOU A MERRY CHRISTMAS

Traditional English Folksong

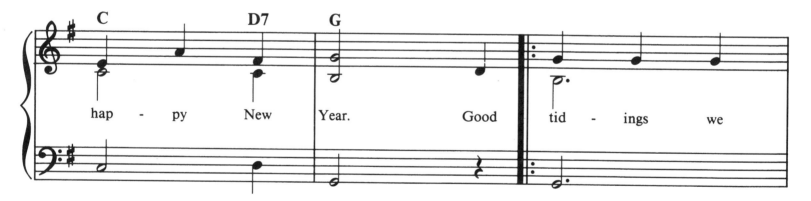

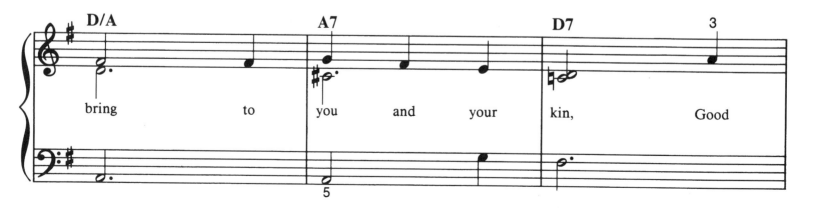

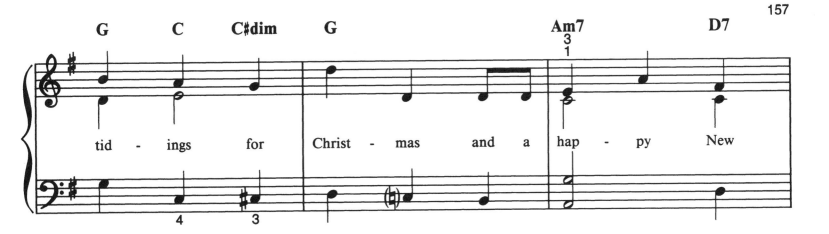

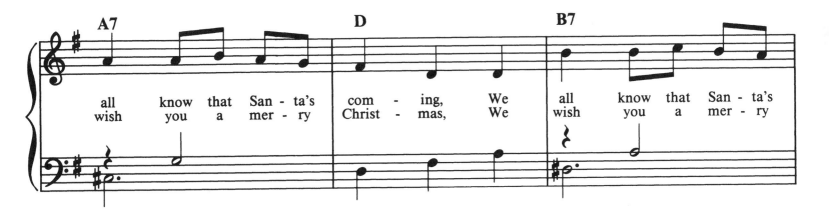

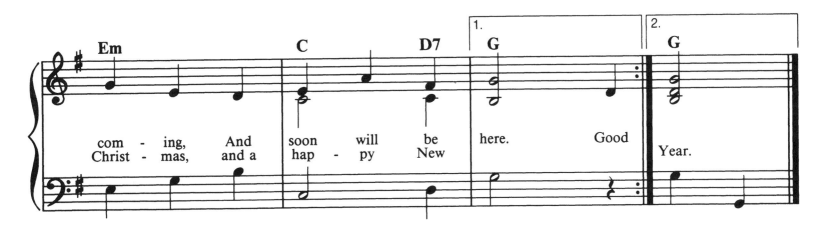

WHAT CHILD IS THIS?

Words by WILLIAM C. DIX
16th Century English Melody

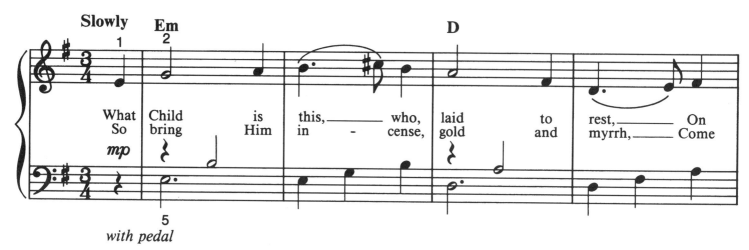

Slowly

What Child is this, who, laid to rest, On
So bring Him in - cense, gold and myrrh, Come

mp

with pedal

Mar - y's lap is sleep - ing? Whom
peas - ant king to own Him; The

an - gels greet with an - thems sweet While
King kings sal - va - tion brings, Let

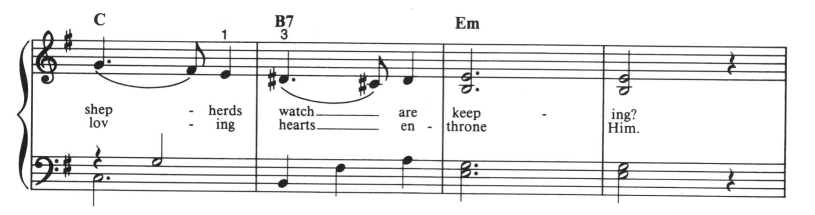

shep - herds watch are keep - ing?
lov - ing hearts en - throne Him.

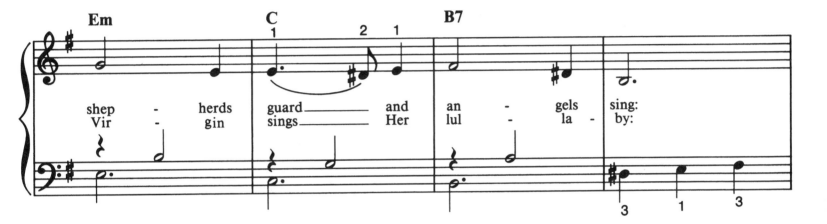

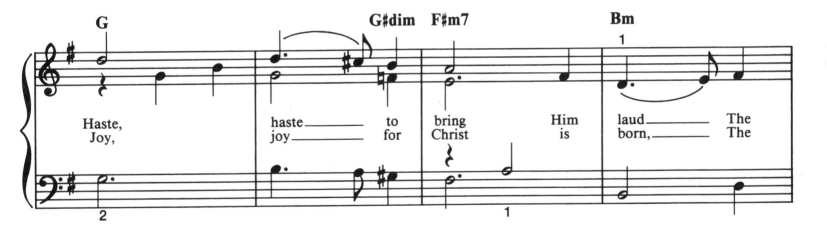

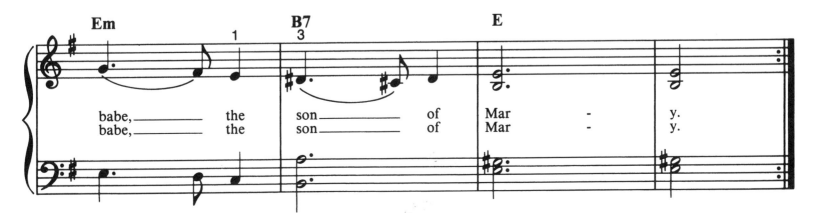

WHILE SHEPHERDS WATCHED THEIR FLOCKS

Words by NAHUM TATE
Music by GEORGE FRIDERIC HANDEL

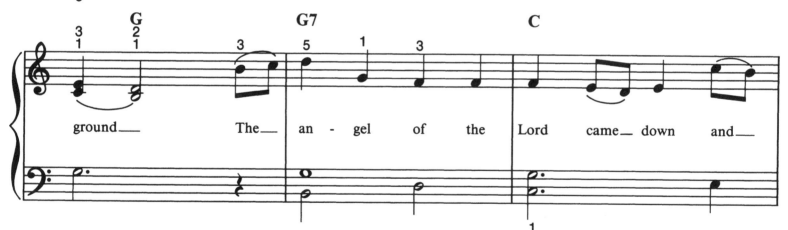